RECEIVING
THE DAY

RECEIVING THE DAY

Christian Practices for Opening the Gift of Time

❖

Dorothy C. Bass

Jossey-Bass Publishers
SAN FRANCISCO

Published by Jossey-Bass
A Wiley Imprint
989 Market Street, San Francisco, CA 94103-1741   www.josseybass.com

Credits are on p. 142.

Jossey-Bass books and products are available through most bookstores. To contact Jossey-Bass directly call our Customer Care Department within the U.S. at (800) 956-7739, outside the U.S. at (317) 572-3986 or fax (317) 572-4002.

Jossey-Bass also publishes its books in a variety of electronic formats. Some content that appears in print may not be available in electronic books.

Library of Congress Cataloging-in-Publication Data

Bass, Dorothy C.
Receiving the day : Christian practices for opening the gift of
   time / Dorothy C. Bass — 1st ed.
      p.   cm.
   Includes bibliographical references and index.
   ISBN 0-7879-5647-3 (pbk.)
      1. Time management—Religious aspects—Christianity.
      2. Time—Religious aspects—Christianity.   3. Sunday.   I. Title.
   BV4598.5   B38   2000
   263—dc21   99-6444

Printed in the United States of America
FIRST EDITION
PB Printing   10 9 8 7 6 5 4 3

The Practices of Faith Series

In an age of rapid social change and widespread spiritual seeking, many people yearn for a way of life that is good in a deep sense and attuned to the active presence of God. This series proposes that the practices of living religious traditions have great wisdom to impart to those who share such yearning. Books in this series explore practices that provide the contours of a life-giving way of life, considering both their ancient grounding and the fresh and vibrant forms they take today—and could take tomorrow. Rejecting the separation of spirituality from action, of theory from practice, and of theology from real life, these books invite readers to consider the patterns of their own lives. We hope they will stimulate conversation about how to live with integrity and hope amid the challenges of our time.

Contents

To Mark

Preface

T ime talks," declared the cultural anthropologist Edward T. Hall. "It speaks more plainly than words. The message it conveys comes through loud and clear. Because it is manipulated less consciously, it is subject to less distortion than the spoken language. It can shout the truth where words lie."

If we could comprehend what time is saying about us, what would we discover? Media reports and an array of books with titles like *The Time Trap* and *Timelock* and *The Time Bind,* as well as my conversations with friends and the yearnings of my own heart, suggest that many of us are concerned about whether we could give a worthy answer to this question.

The hour has come to turn our minds and our hearts to the problem of time in our lives. This problem has been around for millennia, for time has never been given to mortals in unlimited supply, and we cannot prevent its passing. Yet the problem of time has taken on especially startling features amid the rapid change engulfing the world today. Our ancestors, most of them farmers, worked to the rhythms of the sun and the seasons. Our children do work that is shaped by the round-the-clock rhythms of the World Wide Web. The shift from one pattern of life in time to another has been under way for centuries, but in recent decades it has spiraled in speed and scope. Our pace is accelerating. Our hours are unhinged from nature. Whether we as human beings will or can or should adapt to the emerging rhythms of time is an open question.

Numerous helpful works by economists, sociologists, historians, and management consultants have analyzed the shape of time in our society. However, almost no attention has been given to the deepest and most urgent dimension of our problem with time: the spiritual dimension. How we live in time shapes the quality of our relationships with our innermost selves, with other people, with the natural world, and with God.

Every religious tradition gives substantial attention to the shape of time. Christianity, the tradition from which I come and to which I cleave, is no exception. Exploring its insights and resources out of my own need, I have found riches that I am eager to share with others who are also concerned about the problem of time. I hope that this book can help readers understand what Christian faith tells us about time and indeed find joy and guidance in this understanding. Much of the wisdom we seek is to be found not only in verbal pronouncements but also in the shared activities of living communities of faith across the centuries and in varied cultures around the world. When we enter these shared activities—these Christian practices for opening the gift of time—we draw on the experience of other communities while also developing fresh forms that can be life-giving in our own distinctive circumstances.

"What is time?" Saint Augustine asked sixteen centuries ago. "Provided that no one asks me, I know. If I want to explain it to an inquirer, I do not know." Although time has been the focus of philosophical and theological arguments for centuries, this book does not pursue such abstract or theoretical debates; it focuses instead on practical questions. How can I offer attention to God and to other people in the midst of days that seem to be shredded into little fragments of time that I cannot control? Might I be able to keep a sabbath day of rest and worship each week? What do the rhythms of each full year of my life do, or not do, to strengthen my relationships with God, other people, and the created world?

This is, however, a book that invites readers to think as theologians. Entering any Christian practice involves us in the central mysteries of the faith, and we shall encounter them here as we ponder the awesome reality of meeting the eternal God within the ordinary days, weeks, and years of our mortal lives. At one level, then, this book provides a point of entry into the Christian life. I have written it in a way that I hope will welcome readers who know very little about Christianity while also providing new insights to those who have been nurtured in faith for many years. I hope that it will find readers who are spiritual seekers, readers who are lifelong members of the church, and readers committed to other religious traditions who want to understand the wisdom Christianity brings to our common human project of living well in time.

This book is also intended for readers whose initial interest is sheerly practical—readers pressed for time who may even think that what they really need is a book on time management. While honoring the help to be found in some time management techniques, I want to help readers like these see that our predicament is more complex, our yearning deeper, and the shape of time in our lives of greater importance than such techniques can address. We need to learn a richer language than the language of management. We need to develop life patterns that get us through our days not only with greater efficiency but also with greater authenticity as human beings created in God's image.

Two years ago, twelve friends and I published *Practicing Our Faith: A Way of Life for a Searching People* (Jossey-Bass, 1997). In that book, we set forth twelve practices that together form the basis for a faithful way of life during the historic period of social change and spiritual seeking in which we live. I wrote the essay on keeping sabbath—a practice we wished to include because of widespread concern about time in contemporary life and one I chose to write on because I was so intensely aware of my own need for it. Exploring biblical and theological perspectives on the practice of keeping sabbath drew me into a way of seeing time through the lens of faith.

Happily, it also drew me into a practice that I am still exploring, in my life as well as on the printed page. Many people responded to my essay with enthusiasm, not necessarily because they agreed with my interpretations (some did not) but rather because it helped them see that the practices of faith might offer guidance in their own efforts to live in time in ways that are attuned to the active presence of God.

The importance of time in our lives, and my growing conviction that Christian faith bears great wisdom about time, led me to write *Receiving the Day*. In this book, a more extensive account of the weekly practice of keeping sabbath is accompanied by accounts of other practices by which Christian people have sought to live faithfully in time: the Christian practices that shape the day and the year. Together, these practices involve us in ways of living in and understanding time that acknowledge time as the gift of God.

The first chapter, "Experiencing the Fullness of Time," begins with the pain of a crowded datebook but rejects the notion that adding more spaces to its pages would provide the help we need. Time resonates with meaning, and as we seek to live well within it, we are caught again and again in issues that are profoundly spiritual. This chapter invites readers to recognize time as God's gift and to explore the practices by which faith communities develop the capacity to notice and receive this gift.

The central portion of the book explores the Christian practices that follow the rhythms of the day, the week, and the year. A pair of chapters explores each of these spans of time. The first chapter in each pair sets forth central affirmations about the contours and meaning of the day, the week, or the year as they take shape in the Bible, in theology, and in the lives of faithful people. It also introduces some of the obstacles that make it difficult to live these affirmations fully in contemporary society. The second chapter in each pair offers guidance for entering the practice today, drawing on the experience of those who are doing so. I hope that the stories of practice that fill these chapters will encourage readers to consider ways to grow stronger in these practices in their own lives.

The final chapter, "Learning to Count Our Days," considers the overall shape of our lifetimes as human beings. Some vital connections emerge: the connection between practices of living in time and the other Christian practices that constitute a faithful way of life, and the connection between our mortality and the God who is from everlasting to everlasting. Mindful of the preciousness of God's gift of time, we join the prayer of the psalmist: "So teach us to count our days that we may gain a wise heart" (Psalm 90:12).

ACKNOWLEDGMENTS

It is humbling to write a book about time. Since thinking about time makes one contemplate one's finitude, I am aware that this might be a longer and richer book if I had but world enough and time. What I did have was the help of friends. I depended throughout my research and writing on gifts of time that were offered with great generosity and good cheer. I thank especially those who read drafts of these pages and helped me make them stronger: Mary C. Boys, Susan Briehl, Bonnie Miller-McLemore, John Steven Paul, Stephanie Paulsell, Christine Pohl, John Ruff, Walter Wangerin Jr., and David Wood. Each one is a dear friend and an insightful critic. Angela Janssen and Amy Ziettlow provided important research assistance. I am grateful to them and also to Anne Spurgeon and Kathy Yerga, my assistants in the office of the Valparaiso Project on the Education and Formation of People in Faith, who offered essential support at many stages of this work.

I have shared some of the ideas in this book in lectures at Bates College, the Institute for Liturgical Studies at Valparaiso University, the Sisters of the Holy Names of Jesus and Mary (Washington Province), Louisville Presbyterian Theological Seminary, and Lakeland College. I am grateful for these opportunities for conversation, from which I learned a great deal.

Other communities have provided me with nurturing and challenging settings within which to ponder and live the practices of Christian faith. It is a joy and a privilege to make my intellectual home at Valparaiso University, where Christian faith and higher learning sustain a lively partnership. In addition, I am grateful for the hospitality of the Sisters of Saint Benedict at Beech Grove Monastery. Finally, Holden Village has been crucial in forming my sense of a way of life that is attuned to the active presence of God. Susan Briehl, whose friendship I made at Holden four years ago, has been an especially important conversation partner as I developed this book. The influence of her generous presence in my life, as friend and as pastor, preacher, and liturgist, is evident on many of its pages.

My friend Craig Dykstra is my closest colleague in thinking about Christian practices. I thank him for inviting me to share his work on education in Christian practices, for all the joy and insight that have come from our collaboration, and for his encouragement during the writing of this book. Craig and I gathered and led the group that wrote *Practicing Our Faith,* which is another key community whose thinking and praying helped orient and motivate *Receiving the Day.* Stephanie Paulsell, one of these authors, has been a particularly close friend and critic as I thought and wrote about time. I am grateful to Lilly Endowment Inc. for its support of the development of both of these books. Sarah Polster, my editor at Jossey-Bass Publishers, has been a wonderful guide and collaborator in this work. I thank her for her patience and wisdom.

To be an "expert" on time gets one in some amusing and embarrassing situations, especially in a family where time seems so often to be in short supply. I am deeply grateful to my husband and children for their support as I gave my time to writing this book. I am far more grateful that we have been given the gift of time with one another. I thank Kaethe Schwehn, a fine writer herself, for her friendship and for her affirmation of my work. John and Martha Schwehn are promising young writers and delightful young Christians whose presence is a daily reminder of God's grace. They have taught me more than anyone about life, faith, and the true value of time. My greatest thanks go to Mark Schwehn, my husband, who steadies me with his love and wisdom even while delighting me with his brilliance and wit. He is my dearest companion in the practices of faith, and I thank God for every day of our life together.

Valparaiso, Indiana   Dorothy C. Bass
August 1, 1999
Ordinary Time

RECEIVING
THE DAY

Chapter 1

EXPERIENCING THE FULLNESS OF TIME

In the Midwestern town where I live, all the children are required to buy datebooks at the beginning of fourth grade. Not just the little pamphlet calendars printed by greeting card companies, like the ones in which I recorded my friends' birthdays as a child. And not grids on which to write class times and assignments. But datebooks, like the ones business executives often carry.

Three decades of keeping datebooks of my own make me suspicious of this policy. It's not that I have anything against datebooks, for certain purposes. Mine helps me remember when I'm supposed to meet a colleague or see the dentist or send in a report. It jogs my memory, and it decreases the likelihood that I will agree to be in two places at the same time. But a datebook can also become the focus of tension and strain, as it is in those moments when I hold it, pen in hand, realizing that to be in two places at the same time is exactly what someone is demanding of me. Moreover, the flat pages of a datebook can become a template not simply for organizing time but also for visualizing what time is: a sequence of little boxes, each waiting to be filled. As the owner of this time, I imagine, my role is to look down on these boxes from above and determine what goes where. Being busy enough to need a book with larger pages is a sign of success. Being deliberate enough to block out certain boxes for reading, exercise, or family is a sign of wisdom.

In fact, we live not outside and above time but within it. Nature and culture craft its units—days, weeks, and years—and how many of these we will finally have is not up to us. Time is a given, and time is a gift. We receive it in increments that flow from the future into the past, a certain number of hours each day, a certain number of days each year, a certain span of life whose duration we do not know in advance. Making good use of the time we are given is important, to be sure, and datebooks and other aids help us to do this. But when our emphasis on using time displaces our awareness of time as gift, we find that we are not so much using time as permitting time to use us.

This is what is happening to more and more of us, more and more often. These days, it can seem that time itself is out of kilter. Grave imbalances exist for almost everyone. Some people are vastly overworked and vastly overpaid, others work too long and earn too little, and others work seldom, if at all. And however much or little we work, the time we do have is losing its shape as round-the-clock employment, shopping, and entertainment blur the boundaries between one season and another, between day and night. No wonder we turn to our datebooks in the hope that they can help us get back in control. When we require them of fourth graders, what are we communicating to them about the society in which they live? Are we preparing them to enter an economy that intends to squeeze every minute out of them, sooner or later?

Historians, economists, and sociologists are trying to understand how this system came into being, and some of them are even proposing ways in which the structures of the workplace might be changed to correct its imbalances. Our trouble with time goes much deeper than the social sciences can fathom, however. At the heart of our attitudes and experience of time are issues of identity and conscience, matters of the spirit. I think of a good friend who had a day off, a precious open day in which she could do whatever she chose, or nothing at all. When her husband came home, there she was with her feet up, reading a magazine. He was happy for her, but she was embarrassed. And so she leaped to her feet, explaining that before this quiet interlude she had done the laundry, made some important phone calls, and helped with their daughter's homework. "Congratulations," he chuckled. "You have earned the air you breathe. Now sit back down!"

Time, my friend had said, though not in so many words, is there to be "used." Having "wasted" it, she felt guilty. Happily, her husband's gracious remark let her enjoy the rest of that day. But for her, as for so many of us, time continues to be a source not only of pressure but also of guilt and judgment. We forget how to luxuriate in time that is not filled with tasks. We delude ourselves into believing that if we can just get everything done, if we can only tie up all the loose ends, if we can even once get ahead of the crush, we will prove our worth and establish ourselves in safety.

Our problem with time is social, cultural, and economic, to be sure. But it is also a spiritual problem, one that runs right to the core of who we are as human beings. Distortions in the shape of our time foster distortions in the shape of our lives and the quality of all of our relationships. Indeed, these distortions drive us into the arms of a false theology: we come to believe that we, not God, are the masters of time. We come to believe that our worth must be proved by the way we spend our hours and that our ultimate safety depends on our own good management.

How might our experience of time change if we could learn to receive time as a gift of God? How might this open us to live more fully?

Busy people may think that what we need is a few more open boxes on the pages of our datebooks. But in fact that would provide only a flat and short-lived remedy, and not only because those boxes would soon fill up like all the others. What we really need is time of a different quality. We need the kind of time that is measured in a yearly round of feasts and fasts, in a life span that begins when a newborn is placed in her parents' arms, and in a day that ends and begins anew as a line of darkness creeps across the edge of the earth. This kind of time exists, but we have learned not to notice it. Our gaze is fixed instead on a datebook, some of us anxiously hoping to squeeze

Experiencing the Fullness of Time

into its little boxes all that we must do, others weeping to see that so many of the pages are blank.

Looking at time through the lens of Christian faith, however, we do notice time of such quality. In the creation hymn that begins the Jewish and Christian scriptures, the first act of God is to create light and, seeing that it is good, to separate it from darkness. This is the beginning of time, which from that moment on bears the forms of Day and Night, as God's first gifts are repeated again and again (Genesis 1:1–5). "Yours is the day, yours also the night," sings the psalmist to the Creator (Psalm 74:16). Throughout the continuing saga of God's people, it is on these that God will hang blessing after blessing. Even when desolate and far from home, prophets declare that God's mercies are "new every morning" (Lamentations 3:23).

Through this lens we also discover the sabbath and understand that God intends for us to have time for rest as well as for work. We perceive that even heavy and painful time—forty rainy nights on an ark, forty years of wandering in a wilderness, three days when our dearest friend lies in a tomb—can prepare the way for new life. We get a lesson in how God's gracious arithmetic upsets the ways of the world, as the laborers who work in the vineyard for only one hour receive the same reward as the ones who work all day long (Matthew 20:1–16). While the culture is counting time, we are also seeing it fulfilled: an exiled people returns home, a promised child is born (Isaiah 40:1–5; Luke 2:25–33).

We can find our way into this kind of time. It is there awaiting our notice. If we are to see it and live within it, however, we need to be able to look beyond the taken-for-granteds of our present experience of time. We need to imagine the possibility of thinking beyond the assumptions of our culture. We need to understand the many dimensions of time and our own immersion in all of them.

THE MEANINGS AND MORALS OF TIME

How time is organized is a fundamental building block of any way of life. This is elementary, as every schoolchild learns upon being acclimated to the bells that signal the beginning and end of the school day. Knowing when to show up, and knowing that other people will show up, is a first step into any social setting. Once inside, we learn the details: how fast to move through the hallways, how seriously to take each deadline, when to work hard and when to slack off a little.

Our approach to time is so deeply ingrained in our habits that we are unaware of how powerfully it shapes us at every level. We become accustomed to a certain tempo, to unspoken rules, and soon these patterns come to feel like second nature. At one level, they enable us to get along in the corner of the world in which we find ourselves. At another level, however, they knit in us designs that become part of our very identity, for good and for ill.

Somehow, growing up, most of us develop notions of how "good" people handle time. Where I come from, these notions are pretty clear, even if they are rarely explicit. Good people are not the ones derided in the nursery rhyme about "a diller, a dollar, a ten-o'-clock scholar" who doesn't get to school until noon. They are not the ones who fritter their time away. They don't forget appointments. Instead, they turn things in on time, and after something is over they know when it's time to leave. They waste neither their own time nor other people's.

Time carries lots of moral freight. Being kept waiting, for example, can arouse remarkable rage in people who are usually fairly pleasant. I fear that my tardiness has awakened such passion in the person nearest and dearest to me on more than one occasion. For my part, I am embarrassed to admit that I am capable of both considering his impatience a moral flaw in him and growing just as impatient myself when others are late. Fortunately, I am usually close to punctual, and so are most of my acquaintances. Even more fortunately, our rages are not likely to reach the proportions attained by the media tycoon Robert Maxwell, who fired his son for being late in picking him up at the airport.

"People tend to be very moralistic, rigid and defensive about their own, and other people's, time keeping behaviour," the British sociologist Jenny Shaw reports in an article in the international journal *Time and Society*. The norms governing punctuality are "unforgiving," she says, and thus are sources of both pride and blame. Almost everyone describes themselves as punctual, though they have no trouble admitting that they often fall short in other virtues, such as tidiness. In Shaw's study, punctuality emerges as the stuff of manners and courtesy, of "everyday ethics." To my more theological ears, the words and emotions inherent in this discussion also ring with the overtones of sin and salvation, of judgment and grace.

Grace can seem in short supply indeed once we begin to think that whoever "uses time well" is right with God and that whoever "wastes" time is committing sin. This judgment is not unfamiliar on the American cultural and political landscape. Often called "the Protestant ethic," this attitude holds that work and worthiness go hand in hand, not only in human eyes but in God's. This label is incongruous, since the Protestant movement actually began with the insistence that God's favor is a free gift. Such a gift can seem too good to be true, however, whether we are Protestants or not, and thus many of us try to attract God's favor by putting our virtue and hard work on display. When we get caught up in this effort, it can seem that success in work is the proof that we have succeeded in our faith as well. I wonder, however, what kind of faith this is: where are love and trust and forgiveness, even for the "successful"? And I worry about the shadow side of this ethic, which heaps condemnation on those who fail to prosper, whether by their own doing or not.

Cultural differences also fuel confusion and condemnation. Everyday approaches to time vary immensely from one place to another. Robert Levine, a social psychologist, learned this when teaching a summer course at a university in Brazil. Upon his arrival in Rio, he made an appointment with his department head and, naturally, got to her office on time. He was surprised and chagrined, however, that she showed up forty minutes late. Then she delayed their conversation for an additional ten minutes, only to cut it short soon after it began because she had to go to another meeting set for the same time. This behavior on the part of a pleasant and well-regarded person puzzled Levine as much as it angered him. Later that day, his puzzlement intensified as several students lingered in his own office far past the appointed end of their meeting time. Still later, a prospective landlord kept him waiting and then broke off their negotiations when Levine expressed his dismay.

Time, Levine realized, ran differently in Brazil than it did in California. The question was, how differently? On a subsequent trip around the world, the basis for his book *A Geography of Time,* he found patterns as diverse as the countries he visited, each governed by rules hidden deep in the unexamined consciousness of its citizens. His own understanding of what time people should arrive and how long they should stay, Levine came to see, was not "right," as if it were engraved in the book of nature. It was, rather, part of the grammar of his own culture.

Sometimes it takes a visit to a faraway place to help us see how peculiar our own timeways are. But sometimes we can learn this simply by going next door. Two churches in my hometown, located just a few blocks apart, speak time in quite different accents. At one, folks get there when they can, and worship takes as long as it needs to. At the other, people notice (and vaguely disparage) latecomers, and many start to fidget if it looks like the service may run a little longer than its allotted hour. My native culture makes my way with time closer to that of the second congregation; I confess that I have even fidgeted, on occasion, when a service there runs "too long." And so when I first attended the more laid-back congregation, my first impulse was to pass judgment on its ways with time—to frown on someone who was late or fretfully to wish that things would hurry on to a timely benediction. It did not take me long to figure out that these thoughts violated the culture of that place. What did take me quite a while was figuring out that my more hurried ways seemed odd, even wrong, to the people gathered there.

Sharing time at a particular pace had formed each congregation in a particular style of living. More important, sharing time had provided each with the basic ingredient of shared living itself, making it possible for each to become a community. Without sharing time, and sharing it in sufficient amounts to let community take root and grow, it is impossible to share a common life with other people. When time is withheld, community withers.

Late one December, our next-door neighbors invited us and the others on our block to an open house. About half of us were fairly new to the area; the other half, including our hosts, had lived there for more than three decades. I think they wanted to tell us newcomers about the warmth and friendship that had run up and down our street as children ran from yard to yard while their parents partied on one of the patios. Every summer weekend, a volleyball net went up on the back lot. The snapshots they showed us portrayed their younger selves, arms linked and faces shining. Our new neighbors wanted us to know about this, even if the hectic pace of life in the 1990s made it unlikely that they, or we, could know it now.

This story makes me sad, though in truth only a little sad, since we have other friends not too far from this street with whom we play an occasional game of volleyball even now. But evidence that what has happened on our block is part of a widespread trend—that people in many places and across many economic levels no longer spend much time with their neighbors—awakens a greater sadness. It signals a worrisome loss of community on a larger scale. It is one more sign that the whole society has less glue than it used to have, less than it needs.

Deficits of time can also weaken the first, basic community of life and sometimes break it. Time for family is something most people say they crave but feel they have too little of, and they are worried what effect this is having. Will their children abandon the family's ways—the values, tastes, and habits that shape its life as a little community—for the ways of those with whom they spend more time? Will all members of the family attend to and nurture one another? Will the adults abandon one another? A recent study of the men and women who work for a large corporation reports that most find more warmth and shared purpose—more community—on the job than at home. Hours spent at each place are part of the reason. The amount and kind of time spent with others, the company we keep, are crucial to our sense of who we are and where we belong. When they change, so do we.

So much is at stake in the pace and patterns of our lives in time, whether they follow rhythms familiar since childhood or are forged in the tough choices we must make as adults. Here is the stuff of condemnation, as a fast-moving culture assesses a more relaxed one harshly or as mothers who work outside the home and mothers who do not pass judgment on one another. Here is the stuff of guilt: how could I have wasted this weekend when so much work needs to be done, or how could I have been working when I should have been spending time with a friend on such a glorious day? Pride creeps in too: after many weekends not wasted, I come to believe that I deserve great wealth because I have worked so hard. So does loneliness, when time is too full for key relationships or too empty of companionship. A friend who recently moved to a new city says that the best gift anyone could give him would be to come and sit, to talk of this and that. He longs for the gift of human time.

When the time bind catches me, it seems impossible to come out ahead. I have gotten too little done, or I have done so very much that I failed to share time with people I love. Anger at myself contends against anger at others, whether they be fritterers or workaholics or simply people who need me more than I can afford to be needed. Time becomes an arena of anguish, and the genuine hardships I face in trying to juggle the demands take on an added dimension of pain. When this is so, I arise weary each day, trying once again to pull together enough energy to earn the air I breathe.

THE RAPID WATERS OF TIME

If each of us had all the time in the world, the shape of time might not matter so much. There would always be another year to finish college or to have a child or to visit a longed-for land far away. We could wander from culture to culture, sampling tempos the way travel writers sample cuisines and not feeling that the differences were much of a problem. We might not even mind when someone kept us waiting.

But the fact is that we don't have all the time in the world. Time flies; it departs as swiftly as a bird, and then it is gone. In this lies our vulnerability as human beings. Our efforts and opportunities perish on the wings of time, and so do we. A verse by the great eighteenth-century hymnodist Isaac Watts says well what we so often try to deny or honestly manage to forget: "Time, like an ever-rolling stream, soon bears us all away; we fly forgotten, as a dream dies at the opening day."

Amid mountains of journalism on the problem of time in our society, this decisive reality is barely mentioned. And yet if we ignore it, any account of the shape and importance of time in our lives, and any plan to set the account aright, will be built on lies. Living truthfully, and making the best of the time we have, means acknowledging that both the outcome of our efforts and the length of our lives are beyond our control. Indeed, it often seems that the ones among us who live most gracefully in time, savoring each day and relishing its rhythms, are those who know that their own lives are likely soon to end or who have been spared death and now see each additional day as a bonus. For all we know, however, those of us who are less gracefully fretting over our datebooks may in fact have fewer days remaining than they.

One response to the awesome fact of our vulnerability as creatures trying to stay afloat in the rapid waters of time is to seek refuge in a God who exists beyond time. We turn to God as "our shelter from the stormy blast, and our eternal home." This line is from the same Isaac Watts hymn we have already encountered, a hymn based on Psalm 90, which invites us to sing of God as unchanging and everlasting, as present both "in ages past" and "in years to come." Together with other psalms and the reflections of Jews and Christians both in biblical history and in the centuries since, it shows us a God who exists beyond time, a God who promises that when we are in God's keeping the waves of time can no longer buffet us about. Ultimately, it suggests, time will not really matter.

Like so many images of God, this one is both true and limited. In Christian faith, God is immortal. God was before time, and God will outlast time. But God's immortality is not flexed as a command to human beings to flee away from time into something better. Nor is God a deus ex machina intent on plucking us out of everyday life and placing us in a realm of "nontime" somehow higher or better than what is available in the ordinariness of years, weeks, and days. Quite the contrary: it is within time itself that God meets us.

This is one of the most important affirmations Christians make. This is the mystery of the Incarnation, of God becoming human flesh—of God living, like us, in a certain time and place, sleeping at night, growing a little older each day. Jesus gestated for nine months in the womb of his mother until "the time came for her to deliver her child." He was born, Luke's Gospel tells, at a certain historical moment, "when Quirinius was governor of Syria." Each year, his family went up to Jerusalem; each week, it was his custom to go to the synagogue (Luke 2:41, 4:16). In Jesus, God did not call us to escape out of time and into God; rather God came to humanity in time. Time itself is made holy by the presence of God.

Time is not our enemy, nor is it a hostile place from which we must flee. It is a meeting place, a point of rendezvous with God. We can name certain pieces of time where God has met our ancestors in faith and certain pieces of time where God meets us still. For example, a moment of prophetic reconciliation happened on August 23, 1963, and decades later, generations of schoolchildren memorize words and see pictures from the day when Dr. Martin Luther King Jr. spoke of his dream. Twin children are born on October 19, and the day is celebrated again and again as they grow older, as is their baptismal anniversary on the first Sunday of Advent. A certain season—Easter last year, or this summer—becomes the season when a widow accepts her husband's death and begins to smile when she remembers their years together. A certain year, 1994, sees the end of apartheid in South Africa. More quietly, morning after morning brings new light, and sabbath after sabbath offers rest.

Such things happen within the distinctive rhythms of real places and real times, in Brazil as surely as in California, in the community that dawdles as surely as in the one that runs "on time." In them we see time that is beyond price, time that need not be wrestled with each day as if it were our foe, time that is the habitation of blessing.

OPENING OURSELVES TO RECEIVE THE GIFT OF TIME

To know time as gift is to know that its basic rhythms and inevitable passing are beyond our control. And to know time as gift is to recognize time as the setting within which we also receive God's other gifts, including the fruits of nature and the companionship of one another. To help one another to this knowledge is blessing indeed.

This is what happens in one of my favorite films and short stories, *Babette's Feast*. Babette, a French chef who is working as a servant in an impoverished household, spends her whole fortune on a dinner for a dozen Danes who are used to eating only *lutefisk*. In doing so, she graces her guests not only with food but also with time. Savoring quail and wine, pastry and soup, the elderly guests remember their youth and yet are reconciled to their age. They acknowledge the lost opportunities of the past and yet accept the fitness of the present. As they eat Babette's feast of fine food, they are also nourished and delighted by the fullness of time, by the eternal now.

Such sure knowledge that time is not our enemy but our meeting place with God and one another surprises all of us now and then. But living in this knowledge day after day is not easy, perhaps especially not in a time-obsessed society such as ours. Even when we are aware of our yearning for time that has quality and understand that contemporary patterns and views of time are out of kilter, most of us are so deeply immersed in them that it is difficult to change our behavior and attitudes. The practicalities of our schedules are partly to blame, but so are the dispositions of our hearts. Techniques of time management, down to and including the most elaborate of date-books, can help us only a little, if at all.

A worthier guide is to be found in the wisdom of people who have seen time through the lens of faith and tried to live in time in ways that keep that vision ever before them. Over the centuries, Christian people have inherited and invented practices that embody their community's deepest beliefs regarding time, practices that cling to the contours of the day, the week, and the year. These practices give a certain qualitative shape to the rhythms of a human life, not extending the time we are given or strengthening our control over it, but reminding us, again and again, through words and actions, that time is a gift of God. In the midst of these practices, we also find companions with whom to celebrate this gift, companions with whom to conspire in sharing it and the other gifts of God for the good of all.

Christian practices for opening the gift of time resist the inhumane rhythms that shape so much of contemporary life. And resistance to these patterns is just what we need. Most of us won't opt out of them altogether, discarding our clocks and calendars in a moment of revolutionary upheaval. Nor should we, for to do so would be to abandon a world in need, a world precious to God and to us. But to resist—to lean against these patterns with our minds and our actions, to subvert them, to refuse to see the world as they insist it be seen—this we can and must do. Such resistance does not require allegiance to a predetermined set of rules. It does require critical mindfulness of the patterns within which we presently live and expectant attention to the possibility that God might have something better in mind for us. And it requires practice, the patient learning of new ways.

Perhaps we can learn about this kind of practice from an ancient story. Less than two months after their exodus from Egypt, the tribes of Israel were already growing impatient with life in the wilderness. They even complained of their freedom, a freedom that left them so hungry that they longed for the places and foods of their enslavement. Moses carried their complaint to God, and God answered them, though not in the way or on the schedule they wished. Manna—a mysterious food whose name means "what is it?"—was to be their sustenance, and time was to be their teacher. Each morning, when fresh manna appeared on the ground, they could gather an amount sufficient for the need of each person for just one day, because it was in the nature of this food to require equitable distribution and to rot if it was hoarded. There was no forgetting its origin as a gift: every night the people had to go to sleep trusting that God would provide it once again. Moreover, at the end of each week, the gift was multiplied. On the sixth day, a double supply could be safely gathered, for the gift of the seventh day would be the gift of time itself, time free both from the work of gathering and from the usual bedtime worry about tomorrow's provisions. This was the gift of the sabbath. According to the story, this tutelage in receiving continued for forty years, long enough to practice the patterns over and over while the habits of work and rest and the dispositions of trust and gratitude took root in a new generation (Exodus 16).

Like the people in this ancient story, we need to develop the habits and dispositions that make it possible for us to live our way into freedom. Time well and faithfully shaped will be an element in our journey, as it was in theirs. Such time does not lure us out of our busy days. Instead, it helps us live more honestly and thoughtfully within them. Its patterns are down-to-earth: festivals and naps, certain words and certain rituals, rhythms of work and rest. They are patterns that can make a difference as we struggle with the problem of time in our lives, for our well-being and for the well-being of others.

Chapter 2

THIS IS THE DAY THAT GOD HAS MADE

H ow was your day?"
    The question, asked by someone who cares, is a kind one. Often, though, it throws me. The day has passed in a whirl, and I have to grope for an answer. "Not bad," I reply vaguely. How was my day? Most days, I forget to notice.

A mother I know has a different way of asking the same question. As she tucks her children into bed each night, their teeth brushed and their hair still damp from the bathtub, she asks them a question: "Where did you meet God today?" And they tell her, one by one: a teacher helped me, there was a homeless person in the park, I saw a tree with lots of flowers in it. She tells them where she met God, too. Before the children drop off to sleep, the stuff of this day has become the substance of their prayer.

"What are days for?" asks the poet Philip Larkin. "Days are where we live." Divided one from another by the primal motion of earth's rotation, days are the humble portions that provide our most basic experiences of time. They are large enough to absorb many activities but small enough that we can see them whole. People recovering from addictions learn to live them one at a time.

And yet many days slip by without being noticed. Some vanish in what seems a moment because they are so wonderful. While living such a day, I know beyond saying that it is a day that is large, a day when work or love is flourishing. Only later do I realize that I lost track of the time because I was lost myself, in something or someone utterly captivating. More often, however, a day is lost to smallness. Patched together from obligations, then shredded by interruptions, it disintegrates into fragments that blow away in the wind. I am left empty-handed and exposed, unable to answer a simple question.

Days don't need our notice to come and go, of course. But we need to notice the rhythms that the coming and going of the days establish for our living. These rhythms pace us, whether the days fly past in a blur amid a flurry of obligations or drag on and on while we wait for someone or something in front of the television set. It is from the middle of this blur, or from the depths of this armchair, that the stuff of our days will or will not become the substance of our prayer.

Where did you meet God today? The length of a day—a turn from darkness to light and back again—fits our human capacity for taking stock, our ability to be in the present but also to take a larger, more reflective view of things. And so activities have arisen that teach us to set aside some time to notice each day, embracing it as one in which God is present. In these activities, we receive the day as a gift.

THE GIVENNESS OF THE DAY

Unlike minutes or hours or weeks, days are defined by nature. They are real, their duration given by a movement beyond our human power to control. Hours, which are measured by a human standard, used to be counted differently than they are now: an hour was one-twelfth of today's daylight in this place, a very different matter in December than in June, in Toronto than in Miami. Now we have agreed to hours of equal length. Similarly, we could agree to divide hours into a hundred rather than sixty minutes or to cluster days in sets of nine. But days are real. The sun falls and rises on its schedule, not ours.

Obvious though this is, it is a fact not altogether to our liking. Playing outdoors in the summertime, a child wants to stretch dusk's minutes into hours. Lovers yearn that a certain night will never end. Or—less romantic but probably more familiar—people at work or at home complain that there just aren't enough hours in a day to do all the things that need doing. One of those things is sleep.

When I was twenty, I moved to New York City. Living in the heart of Manhattan was occasionally frightening, but it was far more often thrilling, wonderful. So much was different from what I had known in the towns and suburbs of my growing up: the pace of life, the noise, the sheer numbers of people. And the lights. Broadway was alive all night long, and so were the side streets, as city workers patrolled or cleaned up and music lovers straggled home satisfied by what they had heard. Up all night with my friends, I used to wonder where to situate the pause that happens when one day is over and the next has not yet begun, where to locate the hour that marks the divide between yesterday and tomorrow. Whenever I thought the neighborhood was finally at rest, some sign of the next day's activities would appear: a garbage truck, people at the bus stop on their way to work the early shift, the aroma of fresh bread from the bakery around the corner.

When does a day begin? In the movie *Groundhog Day,* the weatherman played by Bill Murray knows the answer all too well: the day begins when the clock radio goes off at 6:00 A.M., blaring mindless chatter and annoying music into the bedroom. It's time to drag himself to his feet, splash water on his face, and go out to endure February 2 all over again.

When does a day begin? The hymn of creation that opens the scriptures of Jews and Christians offers an answer too. After each creative act—light, sky, seas, and more—God sees the goodness of what has been made, and the narrator pauses briefly to declare that a day has come and gone: "And there was evening and there was morning, the first (second, third, fourth, fifth, sixth) day" (Genesis 1). Here days begin at dusk.

17

Eugene Peterson, a minister and author, urges fast-paced moderns to pay attention to the wisdom of Genesis in this matter. Perceiving day's beginning at the darkening point teaches us something important about who we are as human beings, he says. "The Hebrew evening/morning sequence conditions us to the rhythms of grace. We go to sleep, and God begins his work."

The first part of the day passes in darkness, then, but not in inactivity. God is out growing the crops even before the farmer is up and knitting together the wound before the clinic opens. When farmer and physician awake, they will join in, contributing mightily, but only because grace came first. Likewise, God has been working on and in them, body and mind, while they slept; yesterday's bruises and slights have begun to heal. Entered this way, morning is new, worth being grateful for even before we have put our human touches on it.

Seeing a day through the eyes of Genesis changes its contours at both beginning and end. "When I quit my day's work, nothing essential stops," Eugene Peterson says. "I go to sleep to get out of the way for a while. I get into the rhythm of salvation. . . . Human effort is honored and respected not as a thing in itself but by its integration into the rhythms of grace and blessing." Morning becomes a time to join in the labors that have already begun without us, and evening a time to let others—and Another—take over.

This simple shift in perception is a fundamental movement within the Christian practice of receiving the day. At the heart of this practice is praise of the One who created the earth and separated the light from the darkness. This One is still active in earth and all creatures, including ourselves. Every day, this One offers gifts—life, light, and hours in which to work and eat and love and rest—and invites humankind to join in the ongoing work of caring for creation and all who dwell therein. The same One also continues, each day, the work of new creation: the work of forgiving and reconciling and restoring wholeness. This too we are invited to enter, both as ones who stand in need of this divine work and as partners in it.

The Christian practice of receiving the day calls us to remember these truths with frequency and regularity. Forgetting them is costly. The blare of the clock radio comes to define the starting point of our efforts. An individual's productivity becomes the source of personal identity, confirming the superiority of the "successful" to others of "inferior" worth. In the end, our datebooks become the defining templates of our lives, and we actually believe that we have earned the air we breathe. When that happens, not only are we too busy, but we are also profoundly mistaken about the true nature of things, turned in on ourselves and inaccessible to God and to other people.

The changed relation to time for which we yearn involves a seeing that looks beyond the vision of a society where time is out of kilter. Our ability to see in this way depends in large part on whether we take the time to become imbued with the truths that can help us see through new eyes. The practice of receiving the day is the cluster of activities that enable Christians to offer attention, daily, to the gracious presence and activity of God.

THE PRACTICE OF RECEIVING THE DAY

If you come from a background that associates the spiritual life with calm and quiet, worshiping in a Christian community shaped by the black church tradition can awaken you to other possibilities. "This is the day the Lord has made!" the preacher often shouts as the service begins, repeating the cry until those who are gathered join in. "This is the day the Lord has made! Let us rejoice and be glad in it!" If the Spirit is moving—and usually it is—the worshipers endorse the declaration with singing and clapping. Then one person is likely to rise from the congregation to give a testimony that puts flesh on the bones of their rejoicing. "Thank you, God, for waking me up this morning; for putting shoes on my feet, clothes on my back, and food on my table. Thank you, God, for health and strength and the activities of my limbs. Thank you that I awoke this morning clothed and in my right mind." The specific words may vary, but the point does not: the simple necessities of life, all that we need, are given anew each day by God, and for that, God be praised. The preacher's declaration and the testifier's prayer take a day that might not look so good from certain points of view and name it as a gift from God, a piece of time that is full of mercies, if only we will see them.

The day in question, we should note, is not just any day, or the twenty-four-hour span in the abstract. It is *this* day. Now. Too often, this is the very one that escapes our attention, the day whose gifts we scorn. The bitter aftertaste of yesterday, often a yesterday long since forgotten by everyone else, keeps us from tasting the day that is now on our tongue; I dwell in my failure or another's slight. And anxiety about tomorrow, even a tomorrow that may not come for years, gnaws away at the experience of today, not just once but hundreds of times.

"Can any of you by worrying add a single hour to your span of life?" Jesus asks in Matthew's Gospel, speaking right to this kind of anxiety. To listeners worried about life and health, food and clothing, Jesus shows the birds and the lilies. As God provides for them, he promises, so will God provide for you. Trusting this does not mean becoming a pollyanna; it means remembering to be thankful for the gifts of *this* day, the food and clothing and life that Jesus' hearers actually possessed at that moment, gifts like the ones named in the testimony just cited. It means offering attention to today, including today's trouble. "Do not worry about tomorrow, for tomorrow will bring worries of its own. Today's trouble is enough for today" (Matthew 6:25–34).

Offering attention to this day requires freedom from bondage to yesterday and from fear for tomorrow. Martin Marty, a prolific author and a generous Christian, reports that a simple gesture each day prepares him to remember that he has been given such freedom. "I start my own day invariably—and this is what Lutherans are supposed to do, though not many do—by making the sign of the cross on my body as a token of my baptism." For all Christians, baptism embodies release from yesterday's sin and receipt of tomorrow's promise: going under the water, the old self is buried in the death of Christ; rising from the water the self is new, joined to the resurrected Christ. Martin Luther gave his followers a special charge when he urged each one to "regard his Baptism as the daily garment which he is to wear all the time." Forgiveness, he emphasized in his catechism, "remains day by day as long as we live." When Marty crosses his body as a token of his baptism, then, he is remembering that "whatever guilt I have from yesterday is gone." He knows, in his body as in his mind, that "I cannot do anything about yesterday; I can only do things about today, and I only have strength for today. So that's a gesture, the only one I make consistently. This signal of nonverbal prayer carries me through the day."

Freedom from bondage to the past and from fear for the future releases energies for bold and creative living, energies that might otherwise be directed to the destruction of self or others. This is the freedom that sustains people recovering from addictions: the past does not hold the final word, the future is unwritten, and now the task is to get through just one day. Like Marty, those in recovery learn to say, "I can only do things about today, and I only have strength for today." Some join this awareness to the sign of the cross, others to another gesture or none.

Across the centuries, in countless languages and cultures, Christians have adopted shared patterns for speaking out loud the truth that this day is the day that God has made, a day given to us only once, a day in which we are invited to live in boldness and creativity. Some have chanted this truth quietly instead of shouting it out loud, but the declaration is never a detached description. It is, rather, a response to mercy, a turning toward relationship with God. Moreover, claiming the day as God's reminds us never to cede the hours of our lives to the control of the powers of darkness and death.

From 1935 to 1937, a group of seminarians lived in the small German town of Finkenwalde with their teacher, Dietrich Bonhoeffer. The Third Reich was gaining strength, bolstered by the distorted religious passions of what the Nazis called "German Christianity," and Finkenwalde was a center of theological resistance. As members of the Confessing Church, this small but dedicated band rejected Hitler's claims, insisting that Jesus Christ was their only Lord and that the God of Jesus was the same God revealed in the Jewish scriptures. Later many of them would extend this resistance into the political realm. For the time being, however, the challenge was to endure the pressures of daily life in an illegal institution with barely adequate facilities.

After the seminary was shut down by the Gestapo, Bonhoeffer wrote about its shape and purpose in a short but powerful book, *Life Together*. Long recognized as a classic account of Christian community, *Life Together* is also a classic account of the practice of receiving the day. Bonhoeffer saw that the shape of each day could strengthen the trust in God and the courage to resist evil that were essential to this community's purpose and survival. By adhering to patterns that made palpable God's active presence for the life of the world, this little underground band could regularly focus its attention on its only sure source of strength.

A rich historic tradition had bequeathed to Finkenwalde the resources it needed. That this tradition existed was immensely important, for it enabled these members of a besieged minority to sustain a conscious connection to a vast and enduring body of believers. Patterns of daily prayer reiterated the rhythms of the Genesis hymn of creation—evening and morning, the points of turning between the light called Day and the darkness called Night. The psalms, which provided the words of their prayers, were known as words that Jesus himself had prayed and, in Bonhoeffer's interpretation, as words that Christ continues to pray with and through Christian communities. "This prayer," he wrote of the Psalter, "belongs not to the individual member, but to the whole body of Christ." Each day, they also prayed freely for current concerns, read the Bible, and sang hymns, which "must enable us to see our small community as a member of the great Christian church on earth and must help us willingly and joyfully to take our place in the song of the church with singing, be it feeble or good."

Morning and evening prayers frame the day, at Finkenwalde and in the historic practice of the Christian community over the centuries. But these liturgical acts are not in themselves the practice of receiving the day. Prayer "requires its own time," wrote Bonhoeffer, "but the longest part of the day belongs to work." Work almost always calls us out and plunges us into "the world of impersonal things, the 'It,'" where we and our prayers are tested amid the hard realities of labor and the pressures of life at a distance from the worshiping community—for the Finkenwalders, the pressures of Nazi Germany. There, Bonhoeffer warned, they would find out whether

RECEIVING THE DAY

their prayers were a personal indulgence in warm but momentary spiritual exercises or a path "to active love, to obedience, to good works."

The practice of embracing this day is distilled in a daily rhythm of worship. It becomes a faithful practice, however, when the dispositions these rhythms foster spill over from formal settings of prayer into the other activities of daily life. Sometimes this happens gently, even imperceptibly: I realize that I no longer hold an old grudge. But sometimes the place where prayer touches life becomes the site of explosions. Bonhoeffer concluded his admonition to be diligent and regular in daily prayer with this challenging question: "Who can really be faithful in great things, if they have not learned to be faithful in the things of daily life?" Later, the great things required of him in the resistance movement would result in his martyrdom.

The regular rhythms of prayer and work lived out for a brief period at Finkenwalde have been embodied in countless other communities over the centuries and across the continents. Though a common store of traditional words and patterns has provided a foundation, each community has adapted and invented, seeking the words and rhythms that will best bring the meaning home. Sometimes these are brief, like the bedtime prayers of parents and children or the weekday services attended by a handful of worshipers at a university, hospital, or other workplace. They may even be nonverbal, like Marty's sign of the cross. Sometimes they are much more full and extensive. The Liturgy of the Hours of the Order of Saint Benedict, which has structured the prayers of communities of women and men around the world for nearly fifteen hundred years, consists of up to eight sessions of psalmody during each twenty-four-hour period. The rhythms of Benedictine life embody a steadfast attention to the "sanctification of time," not just for the sake of the monastics but for the sake of the world. Praying with a Benedictine community, knowing that the psalms we are singing are also the prayers of a great chorus past, present, and future, I sense that the hours of *this* day are also interwoven, mysteriously, in the hours of an eternal day.

Whether you pray in the physical presence of others or alone, the united advice of the Christian tradition is this: be regular in daily prayer. To be honest, this advice is difficult for me to follow. I pray

This Is the Day That God Has Made

daily, but I seem always to be making a new resolution to do so more deeply and extensively. What I yearn for, though, is not simply to pray. What I yearn for is to view the world differently because I have viewed it in relation to God. I bring to daily prayer the yearning to know myself and others as God knows us, so that I may love more fully and grow stronger in being who God would have me be and in living how God would have me live. These are yearnings that begin to be met in prayer but that will be fulfilled, or not, amid the vibrant realities of each given day. Bonhoeffer's question about the effect of daily disciplines of prayer haunts me: "Has it transported her for a few short moments into a spiritual ecstasy that vanishes when everyday life returns, or has it lodged the Word of God so soberly and so deeply in her heart that it holds and strengthens her all day, impelling her to active love, to obedience, to good works? Only the day can decide."

What is the Word that holds and strengthens us all day, the Word that makes a difference? For centuries, certain texts have been linked to certain times of day and thus to certain daily situations of need. Two liturgies set at the hinges of light and darkness hold particularly rich insights. These have been called the "cathedral hours" because they were designed for the people who lived and worked in towns, in contrast to the full Liturgy of the Hours of the monastery. These liturgies contain the traditional words for morning and evening, the daily Word for people for whom the longest part of the day belongs to work.

"Open my lips, O God, and my mouth shall declare your praise," the traditional first sentence of morning prayer, fosters a disposition: we enter this day with grateful hearts, with praise on our lips instead of the discouragement or anger we might prefer to vent. Having only recently emerged from the perilous place of dreaming, we choose to feast our minds on what is good rather than on what we may dread in the day that lies ahead. We also get our lips and tongues into the habit of building up rather than tearing down. Then, after psalms and prayers that carry us into every human emotion and evoke our concern for every area of human need, we praise God again, concluding the service with the song Zechariah sang at the birth of his son, John the Baptist (Luke 1:68–79). The song's closing lines send us into a workaday world that is lit by a sunrise that others may not yet see. "By the tender mercy of our God, the dawn from on high will break upon us, to give light to those who sit in darkness and in the shadow of death, to guide our feet into the way of peace." We are prepared to resist darkness and death and to walk in the paths of peace.

By evening, we may wonder whether darkness and death have not prevailed. Mary, the young girl who has just learned that she is chosen to bear the Christ, sings an answer in the traditional song of evening prayer, the Magnificat (Luke 1:46–55). At vespers, joy and praise are once again summoned from our lips. And so are some surprising reversals that put the day's work in proper perspective. God "has scattered the proud in the thoughts of their hearts," we sing with Mary; God "has brought down the powerful from their thrones, and lifted up the lowly. God has filled the hungry with good things, and sent the rich away empty." If we came to evening prayer puffed up by the successes of our day, we are called to remember those who hunger. If we came bent low, we know once again that God is our strength. These words can be pronounced by anyone, even those who are resolutely stuck in the view that the mighty are mighty and the lowly low. They become part of the practice of faithfully receiving this day, however, when they are sung from the heart of a person and a community whose work in daily life has caught them up in cooperating with God to fill the hungry or to scatter the proud.

The gestures, words, and work through which we practice receiving this day are repeated morning after morning, evening after evening, and also during the hours in between. Though the repetition can lull us into boredom or complacency, there is no other way. The days we embrace in this practice are like manna: they cannot be hoarded. When the day brings suffering, enduring this day's suffering, not dreading next month's deterioration, is the necessity of this day. When the day brings testing or opportunity, to meet this free from bondage to the past or dread of the future is this day's urgency. Jesus taught his disciples to ask God for bread for this day, not for all of them.

This Is the Day That God Has Made

CAN WE ENTER THIS PRACTICE TODAY?

By now it is clear that the very practice that proposes to help us live more fully and faithfully in time also takes time. Rich though the Christian heritage regarding the shape of the day may be, we have to wonder how it can become embodied amid the complexities of our lives. Do we really have time for this?

The answer is not readily apparent. One problem that clouds the response is simple busyness, which afflicts people in different life circumstances to different degrees. Potentially more intractable, however, is an infrastructure of time that affects us all. Its engines dazzle us with prospects of wealth and efficiency, driving and luring us into days whose patterns are rigid and amorphous at the same time. These engines are the clock and the global marketplace. Human beings are their makers and masters, yet it often seems that they are ours.

Beaten by the Clock

It is a great irony that monasteries—the very institutions from which we can learn so much about the practice of receiving the day—were pioneers in the development and use of clocks. Because Benedictine monks were committed to praying at set hours during the course of each day, it was crucial to them to discover a way to call the community to prayer. And they did, inventing machines that governed the ringing of the *clocca,* or bells. When the *clocca* rang, they drew attention to the eternity of God and the brevity of human life.

When later set up in the town square and linked to patterns of productive labor and exchange, however, the reliable timepieces of the monks acquired a very different meaning. Indeed, the eighteenth-century satirist Jonathan Swift suggested that clocks themselves were becoming the gods of mercantile society. When Gulliver traveled to Lilliput, Swift recounted in his famous novel, the small inhabitants were puzzled by the ticking object that hung at his waist. "We conjecture," they reported, that "it is either some unknown Animal, or the God that he worships. . . . But we are more inclined to the latter Opinion, because he assured us that he seldom did any Thing without consulting it . . . and said it pointed out the Time for every Action of his Life."

By dividing time into objective segments that could be named and counted, clocks enabled people to communicate with precision about the order and use of those segments. Moreover, when many clocks were set to the same hour and everyone could find out what those clocks said, the life of a whole city or nation could be *synchronized,* literally "timed together." People became temporally accountable, far more so than when timekeeping was attuned primarily to the sun. Eventually, accountants kept close track of wages due as workers labored hour after hour. Tardy students were held accountable for each minute of lost instruction. You could count on when the train would arrive.

Clocks can announce the moment for parties and ball games as well as for train departures and factory shifts, to be sure. But the fact is that they played an indispensable role in technological and commercial development, and they continue to tick or hum primarily in relation to the economic realm today. With clocks, those who agree with Ben Franklin that time is money can readily reckon the dollar value of every minute, if they so choose. Moreover, clock time, which is measurable and constant itself, undergirds a program of measurable and constant productivity unthinkable under a less exact system of ordering hours and minutes. Efficiency becomes first a thinkable goal and then a norm in human work and relations.

When this happens—and it has happened—not only economic productivity but also human relationships are affected. Poignant examples of the results fill Arlie Russell Hochschild's study of corporate employees and their children, *The Time Bind.* The clock-driven efficiency of the workplace, Hochschild suggests, has come to govern not only these employees' lives on the job but also their lives at home. Her study follows parents who work long hours on the assembly line or in the executive suite, and it follows their children, who dawdle, stretch out their bedtime rituals as long as they can, and negotiate baldly for more parental time. The beleaguered adults turn for help to time management techniques learned at work: "to hurry, to delegate, to delay, to forgo, to segment, to hyperorganize the precious remains of family time." Denise Morgan ignores the phone to read to her kids from precisely 8:00 to 8:45. Vicky King bargains with her little girl for extended weekday work hours by promising play on Saturday. John Bell gets home a few minutes before his wife, checks the phone answering machine, and turns on the oven for the dinner she will prepare. Most of these families are holding on, but the domestic atmosphere is charged with a sense of the importance, cost, and scarcity of time.

Hochschild likens these parents to supervisors with stopwatches, holding children and one another to the rigid schedules without which their productivity would be impossible. The image is one of a factory, the site of the clock's most rigid control of human effort. Resisting such control, wherever human beings cry out for relief, is essential to any contemporary effort to enter the Christian practice of receiving the day.

Adrift on a Sea of Time

Throughout human history, most people have slept by night and worked by day. We human beings are adaptive, however, and always have been. Every night for thousands of years has seen humans keeping watch and hunting, nursing the ill and nursing babies, feeding the fire and setting out the dough to rise. Festivals and emergencies overturn the boundaries between day and night as well; life in the city that never sleeps is full of both, and even a tiny hamlet is wide awake at midnight once in a while. Moreover, some people just need less sleep than others or need it at different hours. It has always been so.

That said, however, the blurring of the distinction between day and night under way in contemporary culture is remarkable in its reach and power. Fueled by a global marketplace that leaps across time zones in a single bound, a new pattern of time is emerging, one that moves to a digital beat that has regard for neither night nor day (never mind Sunday or Monday, winter or summer). The Internet is both its emblem and its foundation, and e-mailers and Web surfers have been among the first to learn its paces. People consumed by consumerism, hooked on gambling, or entranced by the entertainment industry, and those who find work in these arenas, are being lured into its rhythms as rapidly as the market can manage. Technology makes it possible and profitable for workers in other fields to use the wee hours productively as well. The United States is moving steadily toward a twenty-four-hour-a-day, seven-day-a-week economy: in 1996, only 55 percent of U.S. workers were employed in full-time weekday jobs.

Working days is in no way morally superior to working nights. If your body can handle it—many cannot—it is even legitimate to sleep in several short spans through the day instead of sleeping straight through eight hours of darkness. But the impending homogenization of the hours is disturbing nonetheless because it robs many people of the opportunity to ask one another, "How was your day?" It is worrisome because it keeps people on the go too long, stretching their hours of labor and isolating them on schedules different from those of the people they love. It makes it less likely that we will share stories about where we met God today as we drift off to sleep. We are in danger of losing our bearings and our companions in the glare of an all-night arcade.

GUIDANCE FOR THE PRACTICE
OF RECEIVING THE DAY

Time that is driven by the humming engines of the clock and the global marketplace has a different quality than time that is given in the graceful turning of the earth toward the darkness that marks a biblical day's beginning and end. At first glance, these appear to be oil and water: Who can mix them? If we are honest, however, we recognize that they provide, together, the single stage on which we who live at the beginning of the third millennium will pass our days. Time is the gift of God, now as in every age. And at the same time, we dwell in a society that puts so much pressure on time that it is often difficult to notice the gift.

We who yearn to be able to give a worthy answer when someone asks, "How was your day?" need to develop patterns of life that allow us to notice the gift. This will involve us in grappling with some challenging questions: How can biblical wisdom and classical patterns of prayer help us put down stakes in the vast and formless sea of time that is engulfing the world? What habits and disciplines might help us maintain a degree of freedom from the control of the clock? How might we whose days are so often shredded by interruptions become better able to see them whole? What can ancient wisdom regarding the shape of the day offer to those of us whose days too often disintegrate into fragments that blow away in the wind?

Many faithful people are already thinking and living their way into vibrant and creative responses to such questions. They can offer guidance as each of us finds his or her bearings and seeks out companions with whom to explore practical ways of recognizing time as God's gift in the particular circumstances of our own lives, day by day. To this guidance we shall turn in the next chapter.

Chapter 3

RECEIVING THIS DAY

I n spite of the changes made by electrical and social engineering, days are just as real now as ever. Whether we yearn for more hours or for fewer, and whether we work days on a farm or nights on the Internet, we are given a fixed and unrepeatable span of twenty-four hours with each turning of the earth. In the length and shades of this humble span of time reside regular opportunities to offer attention to God, to ourselves, to other people, and to creation. Discerning what these opportunities are and how to weave them into the distinctive patterns of our own lives can help us answer truly when someone asks, "Where did you meet God today?" This discernment begins with the basic activities in which we have received attention from others. It continues, in changing circumstances, all our lives long.

HONORING THE BODY, DAY BY DAY

It is our bodies that first introduce us to the fact of the day and to its rhythms. Good parents welcome new babies into the human community by keeping them clean, by encouraging them to sleep when others in the household sleep, and by providing food fit for their age at regular intervals. The dailiness, the regularity, of these efforts is of the essence: doing them reliably, every day, honors the bodies of children and also prepares them for trusting relationships with other people. Eventually, children eat what everyone else does and become contenders for time in the family shower.

By adulthood, certain regularities of eating and washing have become fundamental to the shape of the day and, in a mysterious and powerful way, also to a sense of identity. Being forced to relinquish these rhythms can bring desolation. People who lose their homes sometimes report that lacking the capacity to attend regularly to these needs is one of their greatest hardships, one that cuts them off in a particularly cruel way from those who have homes. Similarly, as Kathleen Norris points out in her wonderful little book *The Quotidian Mysteries,* neglecting the elementary physical acts of self-care— "shampooing the hair, washing the body, brushing the teeth, drinking enough water, taking a daily vitamin, going for a walk"—can be a signal of isolation from reality itself. Melancholia shows itself first in sloth about these supposedly small things. "Combating sloth, being willing to care for oneself and others on a daily basis," Norris notes, "is no small part of what constitutes basic human sanity, a faith in the everyday."

Respecting the body's daily needs and making space for their fulfillment is part of honoring the integrity of each twenty-four-hour period. A collapse of health is often what alerts someone who is working too long and too hard that he must rethink the pattern of his days. Skipping meals, failing to get any exercise, even neglecting to take time to go to the bathroom—these are far from trivial. The Rule of Saint Benedict sets forth advice for the body as for the soul, commending times for meals as well as for prayer and stipulating that the monks' day should begin at a certain hour because by then their food would be fully digested. Benedict also allows for adjusting the time of morning prayers in accord with seasonal changes in daylight in order to "give the monks the opportunity to care for nature's needs" between Vigils and Lauds.

The Christian practice of receiving the day is made for people who have and are bodies. These bodies will operate, for a while, on mere fuel, which now can be obtained at all hours from the same outlets that sell fuel for motor vehicles. But these bodies cry out for something better than fuel: they cry out for care, for nourishment, for exercise, for rest. No two bodies are just the same, so each of us must listen carefully to our own in order to discern what patterns of daily life will meet these needs.

Martin Marty, who has joked that his Swiss ancestry gives him a special way with time, recommends another activity that attends to this aspect of the practice of receiving the day: napping. Having noticed that a brief nap increases his energy for hours, he has for decades taken two on most days, and he is glad to teach others how to gain similar benefits. To those who think they would have too much difficulty falling asleep, he offers counsel based on his theory that "what keeps us awake and stressful is guilt about yesterday and worry about tomorrow." Some, I know, have trouble drifting off for other reasons. When naps are possible, however, they provide refreshment of body, mind, and spirit.

We can also remember, and help one another remember, the grace and blessing we experience in the little acts of embodied daily life. Certain mealtime traditions help us do this: right out loud, we say "grace," naming the foods we are about to eat as gifts from God's bounty. The little prayers that ask God to bless our meals can appear hollow to those unaccustomed to joining in, but in effect they redescribe the act of eating. What might be seen as a taking on of fuel is disclosed as really a way of receiving what is good and necessary from God, the source of life. Similarly, I once heard a sermon that urged me to think of each morning's shower as a renewal of my baptism. Though I forget this for months on end, it comes back to me now and then as a little gift.

THE OFFERING OF ATTENTION

In the poem "Five A.M. in the Pinewoods," Mary Oliver sits under the trees, waiting for two deer. She pays attention with everything

that she is, and when the deer come, she sees them truly. Wondrously,
one of the deer sees her too, really sees her.

I'd seen
their hoofprints in the deep
needles and knew
they ended the long night

under the pines, walking
like two mute
and beautiful women toward
the deeper woods, so I

got up in the dark and
went there. They came
slowly down the hill
and looked at me sitting under

the blue trees, shyly
they stepped
closer and stared
from under their thick lashes and even

nibbled some damp
tassels of weeds. This
is not a poem about a dream,
though it could be.

This is a poem about the world
that is ours, or could be.
Finally
one of them—I swear it!—

would have come to my arms.
But the other
stamped sharp hoof in the
pine needles like

the tap of sanity,
and they went off together through

the trees. When I woke
I was alone,

I was thinking:
so this is how you swim inward,
so this is how you flow outward,
so this is how you pray.

I asked participants in a workshop on time where they experienced the greatest pain and challenge in relation to time. These men and women gave one answer again and again: they felt buffeted about by demands, torn in too many directions, distracted. So many concerns harried them that they rarely felt thoroughly present to any one person or thing. The feeling they described was akin to the vagueness I often experience when someone asks if I've had a good day and I cannot answer, because the day is all out of focus.

What do we mean when we say we feel "distracted"? Looking up from the desk upon hearing a child's cry is one form of distraction, a form that is normal and healthy. I lose the thread of what I am reading, but the call to which I respond is urgent and clear. I do not so much lose focus as change focus. Another kind of distraction has me walking into a wall or even stumbling over my child at play, causing thoughtless harm to myself or others because my mind is recalling or anticipating another moment rather than attending to this one. When "distraction" edges us nearer to its cognate "distraught," a certain loss of perspective or even of sanity threatens.

Distraction's opposite, and its antidote, is attention. "Experiencing the present purely is being emptied and hollow," writes Annie Dillard. "You catch grace as a man fills his cup under a waterfall." Poets pursue such moments; many a poem preserves the fruit of attention, as Mary Oliver's does. Dillard, a poet who also writes exquisite prose, spent a year offering attention to a creek and all that surrounded it, recording her experience in *Pilgrim at Tinker Creek*. Simply reading poems or books like these attentively can cut through the distraction of those of us who have no ability to craft meter and metaphor—or no woods nearby.

Frequent and regular acts of attention are anchors for the practice of receiving the day. Nature provides many lively and fascinating points of focus; some of my happiest very busy friends are avid bird-watchers (*birders* is their word for it) who relish treks through forest or wetland with their senses and intelligence fully attentive to creatures whose presence most of us would barely notice. Yet some of the most exemplary guides in the art of paying attention have been drawn to very different points of focus. The French philosopher Simone Weil saw that the everyday studying that students do—learning math or grammar or history—can form in them rich capacities for attention. Indeed, she suggested, this is study's most important purpose, for those who learn attention in this way become able to give attention also to other people and to God. They become able to be present to those who are suffering, and they become able to pray.

DAILY STRUCTURES THAT FREE OR BIND

The Christian practice of receiving the day begins with setting aside a part of each day for attention to God. This piece of time leans deliberately into the wind, grounding us to resist the forces that hurry us on to distraction. It becomes the regular setting for seeing the whole day through the lens of grace as we remember the truths about God and ourselves that inform our resistance. Monastics offer this time in certain patterns; the parents of young children offer it (and teach their children to offer it) in other forms, often at bedtime. Each practitioner needs to find this space each day, in a form that fits his or her rhythms. Finding it, we may discover, like Mary Oliver, not only that we see more clearly but also that we ourselves are being seen.

The idea of doing something with *regularity* arises from the concept of the *regula,* or rule. A monastery is governed by an official written rule that serves as the basis for the covenant among community members, making possible a certain way of life and expressing the convictions implicit in that way of life. Rules do their work amid the humblest details of daily life: they direct what time to get up, how to eat, what to do when a stranger comes to the door, and more.

Those of us who do not live in monasteries also live by rules of a sort, at least in bits and pieces. A grandmother reads her daily devotions, does some laundry, and then heads off to volunteer in a local school. A pastor gets up early every morning to read for two hours, not to prepare a class or sermon but to nourish his heart and mind. A teacher finds physical and mental renewal in a long walk each afternoon. My neighbor, knowing that I am writing about the shape of daily life, assures me that her family always eats the evening meal together. (Though I wonder how they do it, I honor the effort—and the rule that establishes it in this family.)

Lives that are overly regulated are unappealing to most modern Americans. At a workshop on time, a woman described her intense attachment to a rigid daily schedule she had devised decades ago. "I hate to get a phone call in the morning," she said, "because it throws everything off for the rest of the day." She seemed proud of her orderly way of life, but the rest of us were horrified. If this is Scylla, however, Charybdis is not far away. So fluid are the hours of this second beast that that walk never gets taken, that book never gets read, that prayer never gets prayed. Its victims go for days without sharing a meal.

Putting down an anchor or two amid the swells of each day is essential if we are to avoid bobbing on its surface or being washed away by its demands. When and how to do this is the question. As one who has failed countless times to adhere to recommendations urging a certain number of minutes for a certain activity at certain points during the day, I know that the distinctive contours of each life make all the difference. Regularity in prayer can seem impossible to those with hectic lives; and perhaps, some days or some months, it really is. When this is so, remember God's grace and don't fret about it. Leaping to the conclusion of impossibility without really reaching for the possible is foolish, however; many genuinely busy people do find ways to build a period of prayer into their days.

This is not to say that each day brings a thrilling encounter with the sacred. Some days one just sits in the pinewoods, unable to notice the deer when they come. Roberta Bondi, whose studies of ancient Christian monastics led her into a personal way of prayer, tells of her own first steps. Her ancient spiritual guides had persuaded her that daily prayer was important, and she had resolved to take up this discipline. But she wondered how she could; did she have the time, the energy, the focus? An extraordinarily demanding new job brought not only too much work but also great anxiety, and her recent marriage had thrown the domestic patterns familiar to her children from a previous marriage into disarray. Chaos loomed. How nice it would be, she thought, to eat supper quietly in her office before going home to enter the maelstrom. But families are not like that; families are where you show up for supper, no matter how tired you are. Praying is the same, she realized. It's where you show up, day after day, even when you don't think you have much to offer. Someday you'll be sitting there, and something will happen that you wouldn't have missed for the world.

SAYING NO TO SAY YES

Honoring our bodies day by day, offering attention, praying with regularity—no matter how appealing these activities sound, they are also costly. They take time. The question is, which time? Time from sleep, time from work, time from what? Discerning renewed and renewing patterns for our days will cause us to look at them with fresh eyes, asking not only what we need to add but also what we need to take away. Indeed, it may be that choosing what not to do will disclose the radical implications of this practice most vividly. The point is not simply to clear the decks for honor, attention, and prayer; the point is to identify the impediments, even the idols, that have shut them out of each particular life in the past. When you know what these are, you know what renunciations may open you to encounter each day's rhythms of grace and blessing. Each of us needs to explore this question alert to the particularities of our own situation, including the dispositions of our heart.

While leaving this exploration to each reader, I also humbly suggest that television viewing is a good first candidate for renunciation for the great majority of Americans. Its format cultivates habits of mind and spirit that are the opposite of attention, especially when the one parked in front of the flickering tube is also holding a remote control. Hour after hour, viewers lurch from image to image, from story to story. Commercials and scene changes provide the stuff of distraction within a single program, and channel surfing accelerates and aggravates it. Moreover, many people watch television for several intervals through the day, often while doing something else. A recent sociological study showed that Americans in many circumstances, including youth and the retired, have more "free" time each week than their parents and grandparents did but that almost all of it goes to watching television. "Our extra 'free time' has arrived (and then disappeared) in tiny packets scattered across the workweek—long enough to channel-surf but not enough for deep relaxation and leisure of the sort that we do enjoy during vacations, and not enough for social intimacy and civic engagement, both of which are declining," comments Robert Putnam in summarizing these findings. And this says nothing of the content of television.

Sometimes an exploration of what needs to be relinquished leads to a major shift in the overall pattern of a life. I recently rode an airport bus driven by a man who had opted for regular hours and less stress (apart from the traffic) after years as a social worker. Similar questioning has led my sister to step out of the workplace altogether, at least for the few years until her children leave home. She knows that this is not economically possible for many other working parents, and she is grateful that her husband's income enables her to make this choice. Like other parents I know who have made this move, she would say, if you asked for her reasons, that she is doing it for her children. But it seems to me that this step has led her into a more whole and holy way of living in other ways as well. Some of the time once spent at her job she now gives as a volunteer in her town's shelter for women and children who are less fortunate.

This is not a choice I have made; I continue to work both inside and outside the home. For me, the ongoing struggle of renunciation centers on resisting temptations to work too much and to spend too much. These temptations are everywhere in the culture I inhabit, but they also arise from the recesses of my own heart. Gaining time for attention to God and to my family means figuring out where to say no on a daily basis. Few of my noes are absolute, and none would strike an outsider as particularly laudable. But they help me resist, both by carving out minutes of freedom and by causing me to remember on a regular basis that resistance is possible. I have not acquired the technology to read and respond to electronic mail at home. When mail-order catalogues come, I don't look at them, discarding most and putting a few away until I actually need what they offer. I consolidate necessary shopping into as few trips as possible, eschewing shopping as recreation. Each of these steps is tiny, but it is in small choices like these that resistance to the patterns pressed upon us by the contemporary economics of time actually emerges.

Unmastering the Day

Even if we give up television, eliminate dozens of unnecessary activities, and adopt a regular pattern of daily prayer, however, many days will not obey our command to be orderly and satisfying. Henri Nouwen, a priest and author, was known among his students for his remarkable capacity of attention, an offering he gave to God in prayer and to them in friendship. Yet he could write with conviction about the passions evoked by days gone awry: "Doesn't this unending row of interruptions build in our hearts feelings of anger, frustration and even revenge, so much so that at times we see the real possibility that growing old can become synonymous with growing bitter?"

Nouwen found a remedy for the frustrations of interruption in the comment of an older professor: "You know, . . . my whole life I have been complaining that my work was constantly interrupted, until I discovered that my interruptions were my work." For this professor, aggravation about the limitations of time found its healing response in his strengthened sense of vocation. We may imagine that this insight had made him a better teacher or had helped him take more satisfaction in what he had been doing well all along.

I have heard a friend who happens to be a professor express just the frustration that Nouwen describes. Like other conscientious teachers, she has known the bitterness caused by a day when interruptions multiply, and at certain crunch points in each semester the older professor's wisdom would have provoked, not soothed, her. Now, though, she is dealing with a larger and more profound interruption: she is living with cancer. During years of painful treatment and the alternating hopes and despairs evoked by endless test results and prognostic reports, her longing to master the chaos of the day has given way to a sense of what days are, and what they are for, that is decidedly unmasterful. To live within each day that is given her is now her work: suffering this day's pain rather than what may or may not come in the future, and receiving this day's gifts.

The poet Jane Kenyon died in April 1995 of cancer diagnosed in January 1994. A few years earlier, she had written a poem that offers attention to a day, a whole day. It is a good day; she plans "another day just like this day." But she is aware, throughout, that one day such days will no longer exist. This awareness has opened her to see this day clearly and to appreciate it for what it is.

I got out of bed
on two strong legs.
It might have been
otherwise. I ate
cereal, sweet
milk, ripe, flawless
peach. It might
have been otherwise.
I took the dog uphill
to the birch wood.
All morning I did
the work I love.

At noon I lay down
with my mate. It might
have been otherwise.
We ate dinner together
at a table with silver
candlesticks. It might
have been otherwise.
I slept in a bed
in a room with paintings
on the walls, and

planned another day
just like this day.
But one day, I know,
it will be otherwise.

No bland acceptance of death informs this poem. Kenyon asserts mastery of a certain kind over this day, seeing to it that what she needs—walk, work, rest, food, companionship, beauty—surrounds her. Her craft as a poet also brings the day under her control, in a sense, through the creation of a well-wrought poem, a poem with the power to move its readers in years to come. But death is not denied. The poet peers right at her finitude, her mortality. It is in this, not in denial, that the day she has been given—not the day she would have chosen, but *this* day—has become available to her, as poet, as wife, as human being. Near the end of her life, Kenyon and her husband, the poet Donald Hall, selected this poem as the title poem in her final collection of poetry.

Few whose health is good would trade places with those who suffer. The wisdom won in suffering is not ours to covet or romanticize. At the same time, we ought to listen to it and learn. In truth, any of us can say, "But one day, I know, it will be otherwise."

Many of the little prayers that Christians pray every day urge us to just such an admission, uprooting our delusions and sowing the seeds of awareness. A Catholic friend tells me of growing up with a rosary on her bedpost; her mother urged her to pray it when she had trouble sleeping, and she did, with the desired effect of peaceful sleep. Again and again, her fingers caressed the beads while she prayed, "Holy Mary, Mother of God, pray for us sinners now and in the hour of our death." My own prayer was "Now I lay me down to sleep, I pray Thee, Lord, my soul to keep; if I should die before I wake, I pray Thee, Lord, my soul to take." When my children were little, I feared these lines and so taught them milder ones about taking the path of love when they awake. I still don't know whether I chose these lines to protect their tender minds or because I could not bear to contemplate, every night, the fact that they will die.

These prayers place the knowledge of mortality on our tongues. It rests there most easily, perhaps, at bedtime, for falling asleep is akin to dying. We are vulnerable when we sleep. The ill we have done, and the ill done to us, can rob us of peace, haunting our dreams. We must trust others to keep watch, or at least not to do us harm. Once in a while, we even dread the morrow as much as we dread dying itself, or so it seems. We sleep well, as we live and die well, knowing that we are in God's embrace. This is the wisdom embodied in compline, the latest of the liturgical hours, the bedtime prayer of the church: "The Lord almighty grant us a quiet night and peace at the last." At bedtime, we are practicing for our dying, and for the dying of those we love.

What might seem to be a morbid and depressing exercise is, in fact, one last daily movement within a way of living that has life, and life abundant, as its source and purpose. Those who can let go of the day, including its slights and its sins, enter the next day forgiven and free. Those who fear the grave as little as their bed become available for bold and creative living. When they draw near to a hospital bedside or a refugee camp, their fear is not first of all for themselves. Saint Francis is reported to have said, "In baptism we have died the only death that matters." It is, finally, in this kind of confidence, this kind of trust, that we are free to receive *this* day as a gift—and also to receive it as a day that bears gifts, including the gift we become when we lose ourselves in faithful living.

Chapter 4

THE SABBATH OPENS CREATION FOR ITS TRUE FUTURE

❖

I remember very clearly the moment when I first glimpsed the possibility that my Christian faith might be a source of guidance through the time crunch that was my life. It was a Saturday night, and a few teachers were sitting around a dinner table. Tomorrow, we complained, would not be a happy day. Great piles of papers needed grading, and we had promised our students that we would return them on Monday. And so we whined, and as we whined our complaints gradually shaded into boasts. Someone listening in might have thought that we were competing to see who had to grade the most, who worked hardest, and who was most put upon by the demands of his or her job.

That's when it hit me. "Remember the sabbath day, and keep it holy." This was a commandment, one of the ten laws in the basic moral code of Christianity, Judaism, and Western civilization, and here we were, hatching plans to violate it. I could not imagine this group sitting around saying, "I'm planning to take God's name in vain"; "I'm planning to commit adultery"; "I think I'll steal something." Yes, we might occasionally break one of the other commandments ("You shall not covet" is an especially hard one for me), but if we did, we would hardly boast. Our approach to the sabbath commandment was different. We had become so captivated by our work, so impressed by its demands on us and by our own indispensability, that it had simply vanished from our consciousness. We were in the habit of churchgoing, though our whines included a little complaint even about this. But I knew in my bones that we were a long way from keeping the sabbath holy. I began to wonder what that meant and why it mattered.

This "aha!" moment set me off on an exploration of the ancient practice of keeping sabbath. Though I had never used the expression "keeping sabbath" much, the practice was not altogether unfamiliar to me. The Sundays of my childhood, though not governed by strict rules, had the quiet atmosphere of a traditional Protestant sabbath, complete with Sunday school, worship, a family meal, and quiet hours of reading or play. A great many things have changed since I was a child, however, and I knew that whatever sabbath practice I might discover for today could not be shaped by nostalgia.

It is the commandment that caught my attention. But what drew me in is the music of sabbath, which sings of God, creation, and humanity in rhythms, tones, and words that help us know each more truly. Those who know, love, and keep sabbath can join the song, however haltingly we may do so. Hearing this song, which rises from the Bible and history and resonates in our own time, we begin to sway to a beat that runs counter to some of the other rhythms of our busy lives.

Two Songs of Sabbath

Sabbath caught my attention through the strong, simple language of command: "Remember the sabbath day, and keep it holy." Actually, I remembered after looking it up, the commandment runs on well beyond this short summary; this law is the longest of the ten and in some ways the most specific. Stop working on a certain day each week, it says, and make sure that every person and beast in your community stops working too.

But why? We all need to rest, to be sure, and perhaps that is reason enough. In the practice of keeping sabbath, however, more is at stake than that.

> Remember the sabbath day, and keep it holy. Six days you shall labor and do all your work. But the seventh day is a sabbath to the Lord your God; you shall not do any work—you, your son or your daughter, your male or female slave, your livestock, or the alien resident in your towns. For in six days the Lord made heaven and earth, the sea, and all that is in them, but rested the seventh day; therefore the Lord blessed the sabbath day and consecrated it [Exodus 20:8–11].

This commandment resonates to the hymn that opens the Jewish and Christian scriptures, the hymn "In the beginning" (Genesis 1:1–2:4a). The meter of this hymn is sure and steady, counting out time's very first measures: a first day, a second day, a third day, a fourth day, a fifth day, a sixth day. On the beat, God creates; on the offbeat, God pauses to see that what has been created is good. Indeed, after the last beat, at the end of the day on which God has created animals and human beings, the work is declared to be *very* good.

Finally comes the seventh day, the sabbath. Here there is no pause at the end; all is pause, and all is goodness. "And on the seventh day God finished the work that he had done, and he rested on the seventh day from all the work that he had done. So God blessed the seventh day and hallowed it, because on it God rested from all the work that he had done in creation" (Genesis 2:2–3). By resting, God declares as fully as possible just how very good creation is. The work of creating is finished, and God has no regrets, no need to go on to design a still better world or a creature more wonderful than man and woman. In the day of rest, the Christian theologian Karl Barth suggested, God's love toward human beings takes form as time shared with them. Indeed, it is on this day of no work that God "finished" the work of creating the world by wrapping the world in blessed and sacred time. "The sabbath," writes the theologian Jürgen Moltmann, "opens creation for its true future."

Those who sing this sabbath song, opening this gift of holy time, remember that the world in which we live has been created by

God and that we ourselves have been created "in the image of God." Our bodies move to a rhythm of work and rest that follows the rhythm originally strummed by God on the waters of creation. As God worked, so shall we; as God rested, so shall we. Working and resting, we who are human are in the image of God. At the same time, remembering the holiness of the day also reminds us that we are not God: this is a commandment, not a polite invitation. Though we are made to do good work and to enjoy consecrated rest, we can be the makers of neither commandments nor days. These we receive.

The commandment to "observe the sabbath day and keep it holy," as recorded in the other scriptural text that contains the Ten Commandments, requires the same behavior but sings a different song. "Remember that you were a slave in the land of Egypt, and the Lord your God brought you out from there with a mighty hand and an outstretched arm," it says. "Therefore the Lord your God commanded you to keep the sabbath day" (Deuteronomy 5:12–15).

Here God appears not as Creator but as Deliverer, and sabbath resonates with the song of freedom. This song was born as the Israelites stood on the far bank of the Red Sea after their escape from Egypt, singing with Moses: "Your right hand, O Lord, glorious in power—your right hand, O Lord, shattered the enemy." Rejoicing, all the women shook tambourines and danced, led by the prophet Miriam: "Sing to the Lord, for he has triumphed gloriously; horse and rider he has thrown into the sea" (Exodus 15:6, 21). Centuries later, the spiritual descendants of these newly liberated people would find in each sabbath's rest a taste of freedom like this, or at least the hope to struggle for their own earthly share of it. African American slaves, longing for their own freedom millennia later, would sing this same song as a spiritual: "Oh Mary, don't you weep don't you moan, Pharaoh's army got drownded, Oh Mary, don't you weep."

Slaves cannot skip a day of work, but free people can. Not all free people choose to do so, however; some of us remain glued to our computers and washing machines every day of the week. To keep sabbath is to exercise one's freedom, to declare oneself to be neither a tool to be employed—an *employee*—nor a beast to be burdened. To keep sabbath is also to remember one's freedom and to recall the One from whom that freedom came, the One from whom it still comes.

This sabbath song is sung, alas, in an ambiguous world. It is disturbing that the commandment assumes that the people to whom it is addressed may themselves possess slaves. At the same time, it contains chords that crash into the assumptions of slaveholding. The act of remembering commanded here, if lived out in a weekly rhythm of work and rest, would remind those who are now free that the people now in bondage are their kin. Moreover, on the shared weekly day of rest, the whole society would be obliged to know God as the One who delivers people from slavery and who intends that no one, not even animals, must work without respite. To insist on sabbath rest is to give testimony to the subversive knowledge that God's bias is in favor of freedom. Over the centuries, prophets from Isaiah to labor organizers have kept alive the liberating song of sabbath, even when some leaders, religious as well as political, have preferred not to hear it.

The two songs that resonate in the sabbath commandment call sabbath keepers into a dance that embodies fundamental affirmations about God's relationship to humanity: God is the generous creator who sanctifies time and the liberator who requires human beings to deal mercifully with one another. One song emphasizes the goodness of God's creation, the other social justice.

SHABBAT SHALOM

For the Jewish people, sabbath observance arises from the covenant God made with the Israelites at Sinai, which established the holy day as "a sign between me and you throughout your generations, given in order that you may know that I, the Lord, sanctify you" (Exodus 31:13). This covenant still unites God and the Jewish people, and no one sings more beautifully than they the songs of sabbath, the day they call *Shabbes* or *Shabbat*. *Shabbat* begins on Friday evening at sundown. In observant Jewish homes, a woman lights the candles and says a blessing, welcoming the day that is personified in hymns and prayers as the Bride and the Queen of the people, a loving spouse who brings inner delight and a beautiful ruler who gives order and peace. The meal is a time of special festivity; families gather, and

The Sabbath Opens Creation for Its True Future

guests are often welcomed. Some families dress up, set out the best china, and insist on lighting the candles at precisely eighteen minutes before sunset, while others are more casual. But in either case the evening is a relaxed one, a time to linger in the candlelight, enjoying food and conversation. On the following evening, at the end of the daylight hours of rest and worship, many families will mark the end of the holy day with another meal and ritual. Parents bless their children at this time and give them something sweet to eat so that the taste of sabbath peace will linger on their tongues.

Amid the pressures of time that affect all groups today, many contemporary American Jews have lost the rhythms of *Shabbat* or have chosen to leave them behind. Many others persist in keeping the sabbath holy, however, even though their six days of work are extraordinarily busy ones. A professional couple in Boston—he an attorney in a powerful firm, she a hospital administrator—enjoy all of *Shabbat* with their children, every single week. Having warned their employers of their lifelong commitment to this practice, they simply do not allow this time to be invaded. As far as they can tell, all their colleagues and acquaintances not only respect their firmness but also envy their uninterrupted day of rest. A very busy couple in New York has had the same experience. They add that they do not know if their family would have survived intact without this peaceful, renewing day each week.

Others, including some who are finding their way back to *Shabbat* after years on the secular fast track, are more tentative in their practice but no less alert to God's presence in it. In the San Francisco Bay Area, for example, a new synagogue has gathered hundreds of baby boomers and Generation Xers into a community intent on exploring what sabbath can mean for them. Unlikely to observe *Shabbat* as rigorously as the Boston couple but unwilling to ignore its centrality to Jewish life and to miss its benefits, they are engaged in searching conversations with their rabbi and with one another about what boundaries to set around the seventh day.

What does it mean to keep a day holy, to refrain from work, to honor God's creativity, to imitate God's rest, to experience the end of bondage? These are questions that have been on the minds, in the hearts, and in the actions of observant Jews for millennia. What should be done on this day, and what should not? These questions have been debated for centuries in a wide range of cultural settings, and newcomers join the debate every day. Unless they belong to a very strict group where the answers are fixed and explicit, they will need to be discerning as they sort out what makes for *shalom,* peace, in their sabbath observance.

In the broad consensus of the tradition, what should not be done is "work." Defining exactly what that means is a long and continuing argument, but one classic answer is that work is whatever changes the natural, material world. All week long, human beings wrestle with the created world, tilling and hammering and carrying and burning. On the sabbath, however, Jews let it be. They celebrate it as it is and live in it in peace and gratitude. Humans are created too, after all. It is right and good to remember that it is not human effort alone that grows grain and forges steel.

By extension, all activities associated with work or commerce are also prohibited. You are not even supposed to think about them. In keeping with this aspect of the tradition, Rabbi Abraham Heschel, who urged modern American Jews to reclaim the sabbath and also made its meaning accessible to a broader public, argued that this day was especially needed by the citizens of "technical civilization." In such a civilization, he observed, we spend our days conquering space and acquiring the material things that occupy space. The sabbath's gift of time—open, noncommercial time—is the antidote to this obsession with space, cultivating "independence" in those who keep it. With no regard for things or for "the world's chief idol," money, sabbath even provides "an exodus from tension."

What should be done on the sabbath? Specifically religious duties do exist, including common worship at synagogue. But joy in creation is also a worthy tribute to the holiness of the sabbath. The tradition specially encourages married couples to have sexual intercourse on *Shabbat.* Taking a walk, resting, talking with loved ones, reading—these are good too.

The sabbath is at the heart of Judaism. It sings the music of creation and liberation, of holiness and freedom. Moreover, the steadiness of its beat in time has sustained Jewish identity over the centuries, even amid terrible adversity. A saying affirms that "more

51

than the Jews have kept *Shabbat, Shabbat* has kept the Jews." Thus Christians should honor the sabbath as belonging first of all to the Jews, not only in the past but also today. In addition, we should do our best to learn from this Jewish practice, in ways appropriate to our own faith.

Christians are fortunate when Jewish friends invite us to come to a meal on a Friday evening, to keep sabbath with them. On our own, however, Christians do not keep sabbath as Jews do. The emphasis of the Christian sabbath is on the life, death, and resurrection of Jesus Christ. We also honor the Ten Commandments, however, and we stand in spiritual and historical kinship with the Jewish people, of whom Jesus was one. The scriptures of the Jews are holy books for us as well. In an authentically Christian form of sabbath-keeping, we can sing both the hymn of creation's goodness and the freedom songs of Miriam and Moses. But to these songs we add a third: *Alleluia! Christ is risen!* And ordinarily, we do our singing not on the seventh day of the week but on the first, the day when the followers of Jesus first experienced the presence of the risen Christ. This is our day of *new* creation and the day on which we are delivered from enslavement to death in all its forms.

FIRST DAY, EIGHTH DAY

One Sunday, I had a few unexpected hours of freedom in San Antonio, Texas. A conference had ended the day before, and my flight had been delayed. An opportunity I had long desired was now open before me: I could attend mass at San Fernando Cathedral. Heading there on the trolley, another conference participant and I struck up a conversation with an elderly gentleman who had guessed our destination, just as we had guessed his. He had been worshiping at San Fernando for more than fifty years, he told us with pride. We were a little late for the service, thanks to an outdated brochure from the rack in our hotel, and so the plaza in front of the cathedral was almost empty. Music spilled from the church into the bright wintry air. As we crossed the plaza in front of the church, a few vendors approached us; they surely recognized us as tourists, but something in their manner or my mood made it seem that they were not so much hawking their wares as offering to help by providing us with rosaries. Women at the church door welcomed us warmly and pointed out a little standing room just inside, where we squeezed in among the other worshipers behind the overflowing rows of pews. Though cramped, everyone seemed just as glad to be there as we were.

I do not know Spanish, but I do know what happens in a Catholic church on Sunday mornings, and this knowledge permitted me to stop being a tourist and start being a worshiper. Patching together what I knew from years of similar worship in Lutheran congregations, what I gleaned from the body language of the other worshipers, and what I interpreted with the help of my high school Latin and French, I entered into a celebration of Christ's resurrection. Hands open and raised, a gathering in: *The Lord be with you / And also with you.* Heads bowed, a prayer: *Lord have mercy, Christ have mercy, Lord have mercy.* Two passages read aloud from the Bible, including a story I recognized even in this unfamiliar language, then *The Word of the Lord / Thanks be to God.* A reading from a Gospel, which I also recognized and understood because I knew it in English; before and after the reading, *Alleluia,* sung, strummed, and drummed. A sermon, an interpretation of these stories in light of the story of this community, which I read on the faces of the gathered people. The shared confession of our faith, the same in every language, and prayers for the whole people of God and for all people according to their needs. *Lord in your mercy / Hear our prayer.* And then the sharing of the peace. For this, I dared to voice the words in Spanish, as they were being spoken to me: *La paz de Cristo.*

A wonderful mariachi band played as ushers collected an offering of money and carried it up the aisle to the waiting priests. With these gifts they also carried the gifts of bread and wine, the ordinary food that would become Christ's body and blood in this meal of thanksgiving. The priest sang a welcome to the table—*The Lord be with you . . . Lift up your hearts . . . Let us give thanks to God*—and the people sang back the responses—*And also with you . . . We lift them to God . . . It is right to give God thanks and praise.* As the band played, a joyful song filled the church, uniting the people in a chorus of praise that included all the saints and angels and all the faithful

53

around the world and across the ages. The priest then prayed again, lifting the bread and the wine and speaking the words of Jesus, receiving the gifts of his body and blood, and proclaiming his death, his resurrection, and his promise to come again. As the people waited to receive these gifts into their bodies, we all joined hands to sing the prayer that Jesus taught. The language did not matter; I knew this prayer, and I was lifted up when my neighbors raised our joined hands toward the ceiling at certain points. The band continued to play, and after lay ministers had carried the meal to stations all around that huge church, the people received Christ into their own bodies. Soon after, a benediction sent us on our way, our last words *Gracias a Dios*.

This celebration stood in continuity with similar celebrations in communities around the world, on that Sunday and on the first day of each of the hundred thousand weeks before it. From the very beginnings of the Christian movement, the same basic elements have embodied Christ's presence on each first day: a gathering of the people in Christ's name, a hearing of scripture, and a sharing of food. The first Christians were Jews who also kept sabbath on the previous day. After Christianity and Judaism parted ways—a long and messy process—and Christianity became the official religion of the Roman Empire, the first day of the week became the day of rest as well as the day of worship for the great majority of Christians. Over the centuries, therefore, Christians have almost always focused on Sundays in their practice of keeping sabbath.

In the worship I experienced at San Fernando Cathedral, and in Sunday worship in countless other churches around the world, the songs of a Christian sabbath are sung with special clarity. Words and gestures that span the centuries and the continents link many worshiping communities together, even when different languages and musical styles are in play. Sometimes the links are difficult to discern, for the formats and tones of worship vary widely across the spectrum of Christian communions: spontaneity reigns among the Pentecostals, formality among the Episcopalians, order among the Presbyterians—and that is only a beginning. Some share the meal monthly rather than weekly, or even less often. In many congregations, the words of greeting may take a more colloquial form than the ancient *The Lord be with you,* and some churches do not repeat a creed. Yet the gathering on the first day persists across these differences.

When these gatherings are graced by the presence of God's Spirit, something happens to time itself. In the present, in an hour or two of measurable time, those who worship plant their feet in a distant past and stretch their arms toward the future for which they yearn. Somehow, these three times blend together: the time of Jesus, the time of today, and the time of the great banquet God has promised will take place at the end of the ages. Holding hands in a cathedral and singing *Thy kingdom come, thy will be done,* we are in all three times at once.

Early Christians captured this experience when they called the first day of the week the *eighth* day. On the very first first day, they believed, God began the creation of the heavens and the earth. Christ's rising on another first day, centuries later, meant that God was beginning a *new* creation. The future was already breaking into the present, their experience testified; the healing for which all creation yearns was near enough to touch. The seven-day week could not hold the fullness of this time, and so the first day, which embraced eternity as well as its own twenty-four hours, spilled over. The first day, therefore, was also the eighth.

RECEIVING THE GIFT OF SABBATH

Lately, *sabbath* has become the word for almost any time we can manage to set apart for refreshment. I go on vacation and get cards wishing me a good sabbath in the mountains, or a group meets for morning prayer and expresses appreciation for the sabbath time they are sharing. Vacations and morning prayer are wonderful, and they have an important place as we seek to open God's gift of time. But *sabbath* is a day, a certain day that shapes a weekly pattern. Though in different ways, this is true for Christians as well as for Jews. If we fail to take this seriously, we will miss much of the wisdom that each of these traditions can offer to a society where time is out of kilter.

The Sabbath Opens Creation for Its True Future

The kind of day a sabbath is can be glimpsed in a gathering like the one at San Fernando Cathedral—welcome, community, music, meals, reflection, prayer. Authentic worship crystallizes the meaning of sabbath. It does not constitute the Christian practice of keeping sabbath in its fullness, however. In this practice, the songs of creation, liberation, and resurrection spill over from worship into all the hours of a day and from all the hours of a day into all the days of a week.

A few weeks after that Saturday night whine session, I began to explore the possibility of keeping sabbath within my own life. At first (and even now, several years later), just having the word *sabbath* in the back of my mind was illuminating. Even if I was not sure if or how I could or would change my Sunday behavior, that little word stood as a sentinel. It pointed at my obsessions, the preoccupations I could not let go—shopping, housework, work brought home from the office. It reminded me to relax when a worship service that ran a few minutes late caused impatient fidgeting up and down the pew. It shepherded my attention away from bills that needed paying toward what was going on in the backyard, where my children were at play. Just having the word in mind was a good beginning.

Practices are not just words or ideas, however. They are ideas that come to life in the activities—or, in this case, the inactivities—we share with other people. When my friends and I complained and boasted about how our work spilled over into nearly every moment of the week, we were ignoring a practice that bears pertinent wisdom for our time. Even though we have since grown more mindful of this practice, however, we find that it is not easy, most weeks, to enter it as fully as we might wish. We have difficulty completing everything that needs doing no matter how many days we have, and the society in which we live makes little room for sabbath.

The same reasons, however, demonstrate how much we need the kind of renewal a weekly sabbath provides. Actually receiving this gift within the complexities of our own situations will require inventiveness and creativity. With these, and with the grace of God, even our halting steps may fall into time with the music of creation, liberation, and resurrection.

CAN WE ENTER THIS PRACTICE TODAY?

A friend who has taught elementary school for years recently became a principal. "I thought life was busy before," she sighed as she told me about her new job, "but now there is simply too much to do. If I let up for a moment, even on the weekends, I'm further behind than ever." So far, her solution has been to work more and more hours, which means missing suppers with her husband and son and giving up her early morning walks. She doubts that she can live like this indefinitely.

Sometimes my friend thinks that her difficulty in keeping up with all these demands means there is something wrong with her. I assure her that this is not so. Being a principal is a bigger job now than it was a century ago. Paperwork has increased, schools have taken on expanded responsibilities for the overall well-being of children, and the size of the school staff has grown. Parents and politicians scrutinize one's work closely. New information about teaching and learning emerges constantly. The range of textbook choices is vast. Sustaining adequate funding, from legislatures or from candy sales, is always a concern.

No wonder my friend is overwhelmed. Though she will surely use her hours at school more efficiently after she has been in this position for a while, her job will continue to demand as much time as she can possibly give it. And this is not because she is what we often call, with casual disdain, a "workaholic." It is because of the structure and economics of our educational system. And it is because she is a person who cares about the education of children. Her job matters, she knows it, and she is trying to do the best she can. But the personal cost is high, for her and for her family. She likes the idea of keeping sabbath, but she can't imagine that she has time for it.

My friend is one of the millions of people who would say that the main problem with time is that there just isn't enough of it. Other workplaces have changed in ways parallel to hers, and people in almost every field of endeavor have come to fear that a frenzied existence is their only hope. Those who work in executive positions— from being a principal to running a multinational corporation—

57

The Sabbath Opens Creation for Its True Future

provide the most visible examples of the hectic way of life that results, but similar pressures weigh on people who work far from the principal's office or the executive suite. Wage earners in production and sales are lured or forced into long hours of overtime work. People who work in the church, health care, or other service professions find it hard to set limits on their exertions. And whatever their occupations, mothers and fathers hope against hope to fulfill their duties to their children in small amounts of "quality time" and often feel overcome by the demands of parenting, housework, and paid work.

All of these experiences leave us feeling not only exhausted but also inadequate. We are perpetually behind, as things we have not had time to do pile up on our desks and kitchen counters, our dressers and workbenches. With never enough time, we see ourselves as incompetent underachievers. We don't like what we see, but it is hard to change our ways, perhaps in part because we don't have the time, or take the time, to do the thinking that might pave the way to change.

Much as we might think our own incompetence is to blame, the vast majority of people have been swept into this uncomfortable situation by large social forces. The remedy needs to be social, too: we must pursue it in the company of other people, not just as individuals. And the remedy needs to address the damage the present crush does to our spirits as well as to our schedules. We need time that has quality, time that furnishes grace as well as rest. Even though it is more difficult to keep sabbath than it used to be, in a certain sense we need this practice now more than ever.

Keeping Sabbath When Society Doesn't

For most of American history, both legislation and custom sheltered Sundays from work and commerce. Christians reaped the benefits, while Jews, people of other faiths, and the small number of Christians who kept a seventh-day sabbath bore the burden. Today this special protection is nearly gone, as it should be in a society where people of many faiths dwell in mutual respect. In fact, Supreme

Court recognition of the sabbath practices of Jews and Seventh-Day Adventists was an important early step toward sensitivity to American religious diversity in other realms of life.

Although religious diversity spurred some of the legal changes that have made Sunday more like other days than it used to be, the changing economics of time in the competitive and expansive era of the global marketplace have probably had an even greater impact. Just as the boundaries between day and night are disappearing in the unnatural light of the World Wide Web, so the distinctions between one day and another are on their way to vanishing in places of work and business. Sunday mall openings respond to the same consumer needs, real or imagined, that keep stores open around the clock. And why not, from a strictly business point of view? Nothing in nature hints that weeks even exist, much less that they consist of seven days rather than, say, six or ten. As far as nature is concerned, days might as well follow one another in an unbroken chain, without names that recur after seven have passed. A society that is thoroughly commercial, intent always on buying and selling, might assess the days of the week in just the same way.

The fact that society no longer protects a sabbath should not awaken either nostalgia for cultural homogeneity or desire for economic slowdown. Rather, it should alert all of us, whatever our faith, to become more mindful about opening the gift of time. If we are not mindful, the culture will not be mindful for us.

No Time for Sabbath

According to the economist Juliet Schor, the average worker added 164 hours—an extra month of work—to the work year between 1968 and 1988. The reasons: changes in the structure of the workplace and the labor force, both inside and outside the home. In addition to earning a living, today's women and men must also maintain a home, prepare food, and care for children and older adults in households where no one person can efficiently do all of these tasks and often in households where one adult bears the burden alone. And the demands have grown since Schor made her

59

assessment in 1993. Corporate downsizing and the multiplication of low-paying jobs that need to be patched together to provide a living wage have tightened the screws. We live in "an economy and society that are demanding too much from people," Schor declared.

The inadequacy of the wages of the working poor adds to the pressure. Thousands of years ago, the Mosaic law granted a weekly day of freedom to workers who had once been slaves and also to the aliens who lived among them and the beasts that were their helpers. Today there are still millions of people in the United States who cannot take a day off because they cannot afford to. Even when days off come, moreover, the freedom to choose which day to take is often unavailable to those whose pay is lowest. This reality breaks the heart of a lover of sabbath.

It is not always necessity that binds people to their cabs, brooms, or desks, however. At the other end of the economic spectrum are many who say they have to work every day but whose pressure to do so seems to come largely from within. One such person, a capable and conscientious teacher, found a telling response to this pressure, speaking to herself as well as to her colleagues: "Show me a person who can't get their work done in six days, and I'll show you a person who can't get their work done in seven."

Like my friend the principal, many people work too hard because they are so responsible and committed. They have challenging jobs, jobs they enjoy, in institutions that pursue important goals on restricted budgets. I admire them and the work that they do. At the same time, I want to yell, "Stop! Your body will give out under the pressure!" These people (and some weeks I am one of them) need some time off—time that restores them physically and spiritually, time that comes to them on a regular basis, time that is generous with its hours, not begrudging them in small fragments.

This is the kind of time opened by the gift of a sabbath day. Beyond the weekly refreshment it provides, this kind of time also nourishes an alternative vision of how things could be. It sows seeds of resistance to the unjust arrangements that deny freedom both to those who must work without respite and to those who choose to do so. It lets us see that things could be otherwise than they are.

Just as society challenges sabbath, so sabbath challenges society. Ironically, the same forces that make it difficult to keep sabbath also make it a prophetic and relevant practice for our time. Exploring it anew is worth the effort. This exploration will be fruitful, however, only if we resolve to help one another, in God's grace, to develop fresh forms of the practice of keeping sabbath that make sense within the complicated circumstances of our lives.

Chapter 5

KEEPING THIS SABBATH

When we keep a sabbath holy, we are practicing, for a day, the freedom that God intends for all people. We are practicing life outside the frantic pace set by financial markets and round-the-clock shopping and entertainment venues. We are practicing independence from the forces of injustice. We are trying on a new way of life as we begin to allow our weeks to be changed in response to God's promises. We are practicing—pun intended. Like a novice learning to play a musical instrument, we may be off-key at times. It may be years before we are in harmony, and we will never get it perfect. But that need not stop us. Besides, stopping is less a problem than getting started.

During the years since the Saturday night when my friends and I whined about our work, I have talked with many people who engage in this practice in one way or another, and I have tried taking a few steps of my own as well. The forms of sabbath keeping that bring joy in creation, freedom from bondage, and the experience of new life will vary from household to household. Each person needs to consider what forms this practice can take in his or her life, and each local community, family, or institution needs to discern the life-giving shape of sabbath within its own unique context. With this in mind, I humbly offer the following suggestions as resources for this process.

A Rest from Commerce

One Sunday at noon, my twelve-year-old daughter received a very appealing invitation. A friend, and the friend's parents, wanted her to go along for an afternoon at the mall. Sunday afternoons are relaxed times for us, and our kids often get together with friends. But the mall? As my daughter knew, I don't shop on Sundays; stepping out of the rat race of consumerism is an important part of my sabbath practice. I said that she couldn't go.

"But Mom, I won't buy anything," she pleaded. "I'll just look." When I did not give in to her pleas, she stormed for a few minutes in her disappointment, first at me and then alone. But after a little while, we had one of our best conversations ever. What kinds of feelings are stirred up in us when we "just look" at the displays at the mall? We start to want things; but do we need them? Is this wanting good for us and for others? If we were poor, how would we experience the mall?

Perhaps my daughter will remember our conversation in the future, during a weekday shopping trip. She and I will not be withdrawing from contact with the mall by any means. I hope, however, that we can help each other visit it equipped with a degree of spiritual independence from its gaudy promises. It is this sort of independence that keeping sabbath can help us form. Although I have yet to develop the independence for which I yearn, I know that there are a number of needless things that I never got around to buying simply because I would not shop on Sundays.

This episode set me to thinking about all the ways in which time and possessions tug against each other. In *The Overworked American,* Juliet Schor describes the treadmill of working and spending on which we scurry: work more, buy more, then work more again. And the work hours expended for the purpose of paying off credit card balances represent only a fraction of the time we give to our possessions. Shopping, maintaining, storing, fueling, fixing: these, too, absorb hour after hour. Moreover, a sabbath pattern of resisting consumerism awakens the parts of ourselves that cannot be nourished by possessions. When these are awake, the whole week looks different.

A REST FROM WORRY

Abraham Heschel tells the story of a pious man who took a stroll in his vineyard on the sabbath. He saw that his fence was broken through and decided that he would come back the next day to fix it. That evening, however, he changed his mind: "Since the thought of repairing the fence occurred to me on the Sabbath I shall never repair it." His resolve arose from an ancient interpretation of the sabbath commandment: *"Rest even from the thought of labor."*

Trying to take sabbath rest this far would be difficult, particularly for those of us who find that the more we try not to think about something, the more it is on our mind. But there are ways to structure at least part of this story's wisdom into our own sabbath keeping. We can refrain from activities that we know will summon worry, activities like paying bills, doing tax returns, and making lists of things to do in the coming week. On Sundays, one wise woman deliberately refrains from thinking about people who make her angry, practicing letting go of the slights and grudges that accumulate over the course of any week. And we can cultivate those forms of engagement with nature, ideas, and other people that really get our minds off of the week ahead. For my son, that means shooting hoops with a friend, and for me, watching him do so.

Unfortunately, it is often the church itself that habitually misses the wisdom of Heschel's story by filling Sunday afternoons with church committee meetings. "We will have a short service today so that we can get straight to the business meeting," one preacher announced. Of course it is difficult to find time to meet during the week, but part of the point of sabbath is to cause shifts in weekday priorities. In many churches, it is the generous people who serve on the committees who most need to be reminded of this. Resisting the temptation to meet on Sunday would help them say to one another, "God intends rest and liberation for you, during at least one-seventh of your time." Eating, playing, and taking delight in nature and one another in the hours after worship, however, would be wonderful ways for congregations or groups within them to keep sabbath.

A REST FOR CREATION

Jürgen Moltmann, an eminent German theologian, ended his book on the theology of creation with a radical suggestion: "The ecological day of rest should be a day without pollution of the environment—a day when we leave our cars at home, so that nature too can celebrate its sabbath." Fifty years ago, before the building of the freeways and the suburbs, many American Christians might have found in this suggestion a satisfying endorsement of their way of life. Then, churches had small parking lots and served neighborhoods or parishes, and people walked. But things have changed. In recent decades, the lack of adequate parking space has been a significant factor in the withering of many urban congregations, while suburban megachurches have prospered in part due to the efforts of parking stewards who volunteer to direct the traffic flow across acres of asphalt. A few of my friends have chosen to live where they can walk to church, unknowingly emulating the walk to synagogue that is imperative for Jews of the strictest observance.

For most of us, getting to worship, and also enjoying many of the other suggestions for keeping sabbath set forth in this book, would be impossible without our wheels. I wonder, however, whether we should consider the possibility that there is a relationship between the drivenness of our lives and the fact that we so often drive cars, even when we could walk. Visitors from other countries are often astonished at the degree of Americans' reliance on automobiles; one recently pointed out to me that you know your neighborhood differently when you walk it. Moreover, minutes spent walking are open in a way that minutes spent driving are not. The space of the sky and the span of the minutes stretch out, free, before us.

As the earth grows fragile under the pressure of human misuse, we need to consider how we can spend our sabbaths practicing a way of life that is good for creation, even if we cannot or will not abandon our vehicles. Doing this will require discernment, as well as attention to the particular situations in which we live. For example, I find gardening a happy part of many Sundays. But is gardening "work"? For someone who does most of her labor with books and computers, gardening feels like a form of meditation on the wonders of nature, an opportunity to ally with the soil and the sun that is absent during the week. Others find similar renewal in walking or swimming or visiting a park. The important thing is to discover in the freedom of this day a place to allow our love of the earth to be rekindled: to notice its beauty, to enjoy its colors and shapes and smells, and to experience how our bodies move among its waters, rocks, and breezes.

Keeping sabbath not only brings us closer to the earth but also begins the process of healing it. Refraining from work on a regular basis is a way of setting limits on behavior that is perilous for the well-being of the planet itself. Just as overworked Americans need rest, both from work and from the illusion that they themselves cause the grain to grow, the earth also needs rest from human burning and buying and selling. Perhaps as sabbath keepers we will come to live and know these truths more fully and thus to bring their wisdom to the common solution of humanity's problems.

A REST FROM WORK

Work comes in many varieties and can take on many guises. Each of us must determine, in conversation with others, what work needs to be relinquished if we are to enter the practice of keeping sabbath.

Some Christians have been more clear than I am about this dimension of sabbath keeping. Among the most serious of these were the Dutch Calvinists who settled on farms in the American Midwest. A son of this tradition tells the story of a costly but blessed form of this practice in his poem "Obedience."

Were my parents right or wrong
not to mow the ripe oats that Sunday morning
with the rainstorm threatening?

I reminded them that the Sabbath was made for man
and of the ox fallen into the pit.
Without an oats crop, I argued,
the cattle would need to survive on town-bought oats
and then it wouldn't pay to keep them.
Isn't selling cattle at a loss like an ox in a pit?

My parents did not argue.
We went to church.
We sang the usual psalms louder than usual—
we, and the others whose harvests were at stake:

"Jerusalem, where blessing waits,
Our feet are standing in thy gates."

"God, be merciful to me;
On thy grace I rest my plea."

Dominie's spur-of-the-moment concession:
"He rides on the clouds, the wings of the storm;
The lightning and wind his missions perform."

Dominie made no concessions on sermon length:
"Five Good Reasons for Infant Baptism,"
though we heard little of it,

for more floods came and more winds blew and beat
upon that House than we had figured on, even,
more lightning and thunder
and hail the size of pullet eggs.
Falling branches snapped the electric wires.
We sang the closing psalm without the organ and in the dark:

"Ye seed from Abraham descended,
God's covenant love is never ended."

Afterward we rode by our oats field,
flattened.

"We still will mow it," Dad said.
"Ten bushels to the acre, maybe, what would have been fifty
if I had mowed right after milking
and if the whole family had shocked.
We could have had it weatherproof before the storm."

Later at dinner Dad said,
"God was testing us. I'm glad we went."
"Those psalms never gave me such a lift as this morning,"
Mother said, "I wouldn't have missed it."
And even I thought but did not say,
How guilty we would feel now if we had saved the harvest.
The one time Dad asked me why I live in a Black
    neighborhood,
I reminded him of that Sunday morning.
Immediately he understood.

On this stormy Sunday in harvest season, the poet's parents not
only went to church; they "sang the usual psalms louder than usual."
In spite of their economic loss, their steadfast adherence to a practice
that was central to their identity exhibited a strength that makes the
pragmatic alternative of skipping church seem weak and oddly in-
effectual. Years later, the son, though no longer much of a sabbath
keeper, realized that he owed the vigor of his own moral life to his
parents' example.

This poem about the formation of a boy's character portrays a
form of sabbath keeping far stricter than my own. And some of its
details suggest that it is distant from contemporary need: it is set in
the vanishing culture of the family farm and the country church, and
the father's idea that the storm was God's way of testing these good
people troubles me. Even so, this family's refusal to let the marketplace govern their lives inspires me to reflect more honestly on my
claims that I simply cannot afford the time for keeping sabbath.

A habit, deeply ingrained across decades of Sunday morning
regularity, sustained the integrity of this Dutch Calvinist family.

Churchgoing was one beat within the rhythm of a whole way of life. Our rhythms of life and work today are rarely so steady, nor is our way of life so neatly integrated into a whole. In an *ordinary* week, I tell myself, I do keep sabbath. The problem is that there are so few ordinary weeks—partly because of my own scatteredness and partly because the worlds of work and home and church are not nearly as integrated into a single way of life as they were on that Dakota farm. In my family, travel to conferences is what most frequently upsets our rhythms; for people in business, it is travel to trade shows or sales meetings. I try to handle these conflicts by nurturing steady habits for the Sundays that are more or less ordinary and by declining weekend conference invitations as often as possible. I would like to report that I also take a compensatory day of sabbath when I miss the ordinary one, but instead I will only say that I think I should. Perhaps next year.

WORSHIP

One Monday morning, a pastor in Chicago got a phone call asking her to check the pews for someone's mislaid gloves. She found the gloves. She also found the previous day's bulletin, marked to show the exact number of minutes and seconds occupied by each element of the worship service. Opening hymn, 3:38. Old Testament reading, 2:32. And so on, right down the page.

Joyful worship that restores us to communion with the risen Christ and our fellow members of his body, the church, is an essential part of a Christian sabbath. Contemporary culture militates against this, however, both by insinuating that worship is not a very efficient use of time and by importing habits of clock bondage into a gathering where the clock has no place. What is in the deepest sense a festival, a spring of souls, a time of freedom not only from work but also from condemnation becomes instead one more carefully measured appointment.

Some services seem by their nature to invite us to pick up one of those little pew pencils and doodle. When hymns drag, elders judge, children fuss, fancy clothes constrain, and the minutes tick slowly by, we can forget that Sunday worship is a way of taking part in the activity by which God is shaping a new creation. Worship can and should be crafted in ways that make plain that it is a foretaste of the feast to come. "This is the day that the Lord has made! Let us rejoice and be glad in it!"

Just as frequently, however, the problem lies not in the service but in the distorted dispositions we bring to it. These are dispositions we need to replace. One step is suggested by the growing number of worshipers who go to church without their watches. Many observant Jews do not carry timepieces on *Shabbat.* Learning from them, and remembering how the clock can beat us down, we might also declare our availability to God by removing the little machines that link us to commercial time from our bodies, at least during worship. Doing so, we would experience at least an hour within what anthropologists call "event time," time that flows in accordance with the activity at hand rather than to the beat of a mechanism imported from another realm. I find that doing this increases my capacity to hear the Word, to enjoy the feast, and to notice the new creation coming into being. Sometimes I smile at myself when I realize that it also eliminates my capacity to deliver an informed opinion that the preacher went on too long.

WHEN SUNDAY REST AND
WORSHIP ARE IMPOSSIBLE

Maggie, a nurse required to work every other Sunday, told me how hard it was for many years even to think about keeping sabbath. "There was a goodly share of grumbling among my coworkers," she reported, "many of whom bitterly missed being able to worship or spend Sundays with their families." Another nurse helped her see what sabbath might mean in this situation.

"It was my acquaintance with René that changed forever how I kept the sabbath. René believed that we could spend the sabbath working; but with a spirit of joy, we could make it a holy day as we helped others observe it. René was a licensed practical nurse who worked with me at the nursing home. She had three young sons, under the age of ten. On the Sundays she had off, she and her husband and boys were always found worshiping in the third pew from the front at Saint Peter Lutheran Church.

"On the Sundays she and I worked, I began to notice that someone had taken time to put those favorite red shoes on Minnie. Sadie would be wearing her delicate filigree brooch, and Dorothy was immaculate in her navy dress with the white lace collar. The residents who were churchgoers were cheerfully helped to the chapel when it came time for the service. René would go whizzing by, pushing a wheelchair-bound resident to chapel, all the while encouraging residents in the hallways to 'come on down.' Often René brought a special treat for the staff to eat at coffee break. I believe her homemade pies, as well as her love and enthusiasm for the sabbath, redeemed the day for many of us."

I hope that Maggie and René also took a full day of rest at some other point during the week, shaping such a day as a time to receive God's gifts as readily as they shared them with others. One model for this has been offered by Eugene Peterson, a Presbyterian minister, who kept sabbath with his wife every Monday, after their busiest day was over. In all kinds of weather, they drove to the country, read a psalm aloud, and then hiked in silence for several hours. A quiet evening at home rounded out the day. The regularity and ritual quality of this restful time echoed what he was helping the members of his congregation experience on Sundays.

In a sense, Maggie, René, and Eugene spent their Sundays making it possible for others to keep sabbath. Some Sunday work does not afford this kind of satisfaction, however. It is important for communities of faith to provide opportunities for anyone who bears this burden to share worship and fellowship on other days of the week, lest the church match the heartless inflexibility of the workplace.

At the same time, conceding too readily that the economy trumps the pattern commended by our tradition does not necessarily serve justice. Though under pressure today, Sundays have been a day of celebration and freedom through most of American history, and nowhere more so than in the churches of the dispossessed. In addition, the historic movement of American laborers to organize for shorter hours and better pay included demands for one full day off each week. Even when employers make this difficult, worshiping God in one's faith community can be a declaration of spiritual independence from the dominion of ill-rewarded work. Asserting human dignity in this way is, for some worshipers, worth a financial sacrifice.

WHEN SUNDAYS ARE LONELY

Rest does not come easily to some people because it means being alone. The camaraderie of the workplace and the marketplace can bring enjoyment, while the solitude of home can hang heavy. Saying "I like to be busy" is not always a symptom of obsessive overwork. It can also be a straightforward declaration of joy in the bustle of shared endeavors. I think of Ione, who lived and worked at a Christian retreat center. "Do I *have* to take a day off?" she plaintively asked the director.

Insisting on forms of sabbath keeping that push Ione and others into isolation would be cruel. Yet acceding without protest to her desire to work every day would mean missing an important opportunity to help her see that she has value, to and with God and other people, apart from work. Shared worship is an important part of this. So are shared meals, outings, and conversations.

A single friend who has been thinking about the practice of keeping sabbath is concerned about one activity that has been a source of weekly enjoyment for years. On Sunday mornings, she drives from the suburb where she lives into the city, where she belongs to a church where many members are single professionals. After the service, a group goes out to eat in a restaurant. These lunches are fun, supportive occasions. My friend is aware, however, that this group would know one another better if they ate in the more personal atmosphere of their homes. Moreover, she finds that her notion of sabbath freedom makes her uncomfortable when she is always the one being served on this day, usually by people whose economic class denies them any compensatory sabbath freedom. She has resolved to invite some church friends to Sunday lunch at her home, but so far its distance from the church and her failure to plan ahead have stood in the way. In the meantime, she continues to eat out on Sundays. Even though I share her concerns, I am glad that she has this form of refreshment each week.

In a time when social forces pull people apart—in distance, by age, by class—we need to be creative, even when we are retrieving venerable traditions. Since my family lives near our church, reclaiming the custom of inviting people to Sunday dinner is a little easier for us. This works best, I find, when we share a meal that does not require elaborate preparations, just a pot of soup made the day before. I know another family that volunteers in a soup kitchen for the homeless one Sunday each month. For many others, the freedom of sabbath permits visits or phone calls to those who don't get out much due to illness or age. Though the day should not be overburdened with charitable obligations, realizing that there is time for simple kindness is a blessing all around.

POINTS OF RESISTANCE

For many families, the most urgent question about sabbath is this: What about soccer and baseball and ice hockey? John Cardinal O'Connor, archbishop of New York City, recently made the news by criticizing the young altar servers who use their Little League games as an excuse for getting out of church. The *New York Times* visited the city's parks the next Sunday and reported on parents' reactions, which ranged from "He's out of touch" to "The first priority on Sunday is rest and worship; it's not easy, but we fit everything else around that."

Actually, children playing ball in the park while parents watch and chat is a fine image of sabbath, as far as I'm concerned. "Do not play" is not a theologically astute interpretation of the sabbath commandment, and it is said that even John Calvin, the Protestant reformer, liked to bowl on Sunday afternoons, a bit of history suppressed by his theological heirs. A friend who grew up among Dutch-American Calvinists tells me that the children in his family invented a sabbath nongame called "sidewalk tag." You pursued your prey by walking (running was forbidden on Sundays) along the sidewalk (going on the grass was forbidden as well) *very fast.*

Making children sit still and stay on the sidewalk—or adults either—is not necessary. At the same time, in the overheated reality of contemporary American sports, participating usually entails much more than strolling down to the park after Sunday worship and lunch. Children and their parents can be swept up in demanding requirements that have little to do with play, including fundraising and travel to distant competitions. Worse, they can get the idea that athletic prowess is the supreme measure of personal worth.

Parents need to set some limits, and the practice of keeping sabbath provides a structure for doing so. The Massachusetts Council of Churches, which encompasses fifteen Protestant denominations, has begun a campaign to urge parents, coaches, and parks departments to protect Sundays until 1:00 P.M. as a public time of rest. Though this policy does not address every objection that might be raised, it does signal resistance to the ultimacy of sports in our culture and take the pressure off at least a few hours of each week. It also invites parents to think more carefully about how the shape of time forms their children in and for a way of life. Ideally, parents and others who care for children will work together to create livable and life-giving schedules for working things out in a busy, pluralistic society. Sometimes, however, we will need to say, simply and clearly, "That is something we cannot do today."

SATURDAY, SUNDAY, AND MONDAY

When I talk to people about the practice of keeping sabbath, they love the idea of sheltering one day each week for rest and worship. But often they protest, must it be Sunday? It's a good question, particularly in light of the social forces arrayed against it. We live in a society where many people simply do not have the economic or vocational freedom to take this day off. At the same time, the two-thousand-year-old Christian pattern of gathering to celebrate Christ's resurrection each first day is not something readily to discard. Nor should we sell too cheaply the consensus of Jewish and Christian scriptures and traditions that God intends for us not just "sabbath time" scattered wherever we can catch it but a sabbath day each week.

My own need for flexibility has led me to a certain kind of inventiveness. Here's my reasoning: Biblical days run from sundown to sundown. Thus a Christian sabbath begins on Saturday evening and ends with Sunday supper. Therefore, time with friends on Saturday night is part of the sabbath. Ergo, on Sunday evening, after supper, teachers like my husband and me may return to work, preparing for the week ahead. In this rendering, the Saturday night dinner I shared with the whining teachers was actually a sabbath meal, though we should have avoided the whining.

While guarding the importance of shared weekly worship that is tied to a celebration of Christ's resurrection, Christians can and should be creative in claiming a sabbath day. Worship services on Saturday evening and Sunday evening provide appropriate alternatives for people who cannot worship on Sunday morning. Indeed, these alternatives suggest that the Christian sabbath can spill into Saturday or Monday, an idea hinted at by two leading theologians. Jurgen Moltmann makes a theological distinction between Saturday (Judaism's sabbath of creation) and Sunday (Christianity's messianic feast) while also wanting to strengthen the living relationship between the Christian feast and the Jewish sabbath. His suggestion is to let "the *eve* of Sunday . . . flow into a sabbath stillness." As for the bustle that follows Sunday, the reflections of the Orthodox theologian Alexander Schmemann are suggestive. The earliest Christians, he notes, held their resurrection feast not on a day of rest but on the first day of the working week. "By remaining one of the ordinary days, and yet by revealing itself through the eucharist as the eighth and first day, it gave all days their true meaning."

Trying to keep sabbath for one full day each week goes against the grain of how most of us live, and it is possible that further social change will soon make this Christian practice even more difficult than it already is. Even so, holding up a sabbath day as an ideal is important. This gift of time is not meant to be nibbled at in bits and pieces as our convenience allows. It is a gift that has ancient roots, and it is a gift best received in community. Opening it, we find not only time but also the stories, the meals, the gatherings, and the songs that prepare us to cherish creation, to resist slavery in all its forms, and to proclaim new life all week long.

Can we even imagine weeks in which every human being is free to accept God's gift of one full day, a day of sacred time shielded from work and worry, a day that is open for worship, rest, and play? In one sense, our society's problems with time make this seem like a distant dream. Yet it is an image that can begin to take on flesh even now, in partial, experimental, but deeply freeing forms. Imagine supporting faith communities different from your own in observing holy days established by their traditions and explaining to them why you need a sabbath day. Imagine becoming more independent of consumerism and work obsession because you practice resisting them on a regular basis. Imagine how your freedom may contribute to the freedom of others and to the well-being of the natural world. Imagine looking forward to a full day of deep rest each week. As we try on these images, letting them alter the patterns of our lives, we practice each week what sabbath perceives: time is the gift of God.

The Christian practice of keeping sabbath is also the gift of God. It offers welcome, not condemnation, losing its power if it is imposed on the unwilling or grasped self-righteously by those whose circumstances make it easy for them to keep sabbath. Receiving *this* day, after all, means joining in the song of creation, which renews our love for the earth and our gratitude for the blessings God grants through it. Receiving *this* day means joining in a worldwide song of liberation, a song whose vibrations cut through our own forms of bondage and awaken us to the need of all people for freedom and justice. Receiving *this* day means singing *Alleluia* and being renewed in faith, hope, and love. It is the eighth day, and the future God has promised is breaking in. No other days can be the same, after this one.

Chapter 6

THE CIRCLING YEAR DRAWS US INTO THE STORY OF GOD

❖

One of my favorite books tells of a land where it is always winter and never Christmas. In *The Lion, the Witch, and the Wardrobe,* two boys and two girls from England stumble by magic into a snowy forest, where a good Faun and his Talking Animal friends recognize them as Sons of Adam and Daughters of Eve. They are in Narnia, they learn, a land once created and still dearly loved by the great and good Lion, Aslan. Now, however, Narnia is caught in the cold, cruel grasp of the White Witch.

To imagine a year without seasons of warmth and seasons without days of special gladness, as C. S. Lewis did in the first volume of *The Chronicles of Narnia,* is to imagine a world that is frozen in hardship and frozen in time. Evil has triumphed so completely that the earth is forbidden to tilt toward the sun. Creation can bring forth no shoot or flower, and creatures are denied the smells and colors and tastes of new life. They wait and wait, but nothing happens. Advent is endless. Life is all fasting, with never a feast.

Narnia's opposite is another land of talking animals, a land imagined by Walt Disney and now open for business in Florida, California, Japan, and France. I visited the Florida incarnation of this land one January with my children and my parents. It was great fun. We feasted and feasted, on sweets and rides and parades. Toys and trinkets glittered in countless windows along the streets, so abundant as to put Santa's workshop to shame. The air was a little chilly, but not too chilly to use the hot tub on the patio outside our room. Winter it was not, at least not to this Midwesterner. It was as if the wardrobe door had opened onto a land where it is always Christmas and never winter.

Though Walt Disney World and captive Narnia are utterly different, they are alike in this: in both places, days follow one another without meaning. They are all the same. The White Witch allows no sabbath rest, and Mickey Mouse is always on a working vacation. The dance of sun and earth between solstice and equinox is stilled, and the seasons stop. The music of rejoicing is either completely silent or so loud as to grow tiresome. The food has little taste after a while. In neither place can anyone flourish for long—not people, not fauns, not animals. Aslan, knowing this, would arrive to free Narnia, setting its seasons in motion once again.

Happily, our home is a planet where the days begin to grow longer in the northern hemisphere just as Christmas arrives. Six months later, they start growing shorter again. Spring comes to every clime, however different it may appear in Norway, New Zealand, and Ecuador, and so does autumn. Human beings respond by elaborating on nature's turnings: in every age and place, we develop seasonal rhythms of planting and reaping, of fasting and feasting, of letting go and starting afresh. These rhythms run through the days and the weeks, stitching them together until they come full circle over the course of a year.

Within the rhythms that encircle a year lived in Christian faith, season also follows season. The natural tilts and turns of the northern hemisphere, where the Christian seasons of faith originated, set the stage: Easter follows the vernal equinox, Christmas the winter solstice. But the larger motions that govern these seasons belong to the story of God—a story in which nature is present but one that nature does not write. Amazingly, even though this story began before time itself and reaches beyond the end of time, it is a story that has room in its narrative for each individual who encounters it in the present day. Within the Christian practice of living through the year, the gift of time becomes a means of entry into this story, a mysterious opening into participation in the life of God.

THE MOTIONS OF THE YEARS

Like the orbit whose span they measure, years are round. Each one begins at a certain point and arrives back at that point before it can run its course once more. It forms a circle. Lay one year on top of another, however, or tens on top of tens, and a thick line comes into view. This line runs from long ago toward a distant future.

Years possess, each one, a certain aesthetic completeness. Each round year gathers the days, seeing to it that they add up to something. But what of this line? What is to gather this long series of years, what is to help us understand its span and shape? I remember a song that depicts the seasons as going round and round like a carousel. It offers a pretty image of circularity and completion. The riders, however, are captives on the carousel's painted ponies. They are going nowhere; hope and freedom are absent, and even the fun of riding cannot last for long. In the song, the stages of a human life are like the seasons of the year, smoothly succeeding one another until the last verse puts an end to them.

The spinning of the seasons, the marching onward of a thick line of years—these are powerful forces. Sometimes their pace slows to a cruel plodding: a year of chemotherapy seems to take forever, and so does a year of mourning or a first year away from home when school or work is not going well. But often the tempo quickens, and years fly past. It is only yesterday that he was a little boy, we think, we parents and godparents, we uncles and aunts; now he counts his age in decades. Where did the years go?

He who was once that little boy can tell us where they went by telling us his story. He can offer a narrative of what he has learned and how he has learned it, of friends he has had or missed having, of illness and health and accident and escape. This story recounts his years. If we listen closely, we can also hear in it the echoes of larger stories. He was the first in his family to attend college, he says. He has flourished economically, but he still grieves the loss of his brother, who was killed in Vietnam.

In the stories of our lives, a thick, inky line of years is scripted into meaningful curves. Like all stories, these turn and twist; they have high points and low points. Remembering and telling them, at least we know for certain that all days are not the same. We sense that our years do add up to something, even if we are not quite clear about what that something is. We also see that our individual stories are part of the grand narratives of human history. We realize that we would not wish to live in a land where it is always Christmas and never winter any more than we would wish to live in a frozen place where celebrations are forbidden: we want a story, with a plot that allows for growing and outgrowing, a plot with room for change and an ending that satisfies.

Often, however, we feel as if our storytelling has been stopped in midchapter. We cannot figure out how to weave episodes of un-speakable pain into narratives that would be false without them, or we find that the plots that most interest us are coming to an end all too soon. Events have twisted the inky line of years into a script we are reluctant to claim as our own or have smudged it beyond legibility. Sometimes the thick line just lies there, flat. Our hopes recede into the past, and we peer into a murky future.

But what of the roundness that embraces the line, the circle formed by each year in its turn, the ring that gives the points on the line a third dimension in which to dwell? Can the completeness of that circle lend its wholeness to lines that are twisted and smudged? Those who worship God within the rhythms of the Christian year would say yes. In the Christian practice of living through the year, recurring patterns of longing and fulfillment, of repentance and grace, encircle us again and again as we encounter different dimensions of the mystery of God at each point in time, all year long. Over time, the round years accumulate into a thick line, and we find that we have been caught up in the story of God.

THE EMBRACE OF THE CHRISTIAN YEAR

When I was thirty, the story that was my life took a painful turn. I was abandoned by the person most important to me. All that I had been anticipating—love, home, children—was taken away, and I was alone, disdained by the one I loved, by myself—indeed, so it seemed in my shame, by everyone. Even the roundness of the year seemed a curse, for what it brought was one more birthday when already I had had too many. The ticking of my biological clock drowned out the kind chorus of friends who sang to my happiness.

Slowly, however, I began to feel the embrace of another circling year, the year as it is lived by Christian people at worship. It first opened its arms to me in the basement of a church in downtown Boston. It was the eve of Good Friday, the Thursday night that Christians call Maundy, an antique word related to *mandate* that reminds us that on this night Jesus commanded his disciples to love one another. I had been very involved in this church for several years; part of my grief was that soon I would be leaving it, as I carried my solitude off to school the following fall. For me, this had been a place from which to advocate on behalf of others—the homeless people who panhandled at its doors, the women treated unjustly by higher church structures, the victims of American foreign policy. I did not really know until this night, however, that this was a place that existed, also, on behalf of me.

As Jesus and his disciples had done, we gathered for a meal. The tables were long, the kind easily folded and stored, covered with white paper torn from big rolls and secured with tape. A candle was on each table, and along the wall more tables held the food we had brought, dozens of casseroles and salads and desserts. I doubt that I ate much, and I don't remember exactly how the worship service began except that it began while we were still at table. Though this bit of memory is lost, however, I am quite sure what story was told, for I had heard the same story on that night every year since childhood. It was the story of Jesus' last supper. As he ate the Passover meal with his disciples, he told them that one of them would betray him. Then, when they had finished the meal, he took bread and gave

The Circling Year Draws Us into the Story of God

thanks and broke it and gave it to them. This is my body, he said; it is given for you. Then he took a cup of wine and blessed it and gave it to them. This is the cup of the new covenant, he said; it is my blood poured out for the forgiveness of sins. When you eat, remember me, and look ahead to the time when we will eat together in the realm of God. They sang a hymn and went outside, to a nearby garden. A few hours later, he was arrested, tried, and sentenced to die.

This is a story heard best, perhaps, in the shadows of a dimly lit basement. I had heard it many times before, but for this telling I had acquired sharper ears with which to hear, and more of my self was listening. Jesus was betrayed by one with whom he had eaten every day. Betrayed. I had entered the story's darkness, and it had met and matched my own. Eating the bread and wine that we passed from hand to hand, I began to cry.

Most of those around me looked away; they were embarrassed, I now realize, though at the time I thought that they were on the side of my betrayer. My friend Lynn saw me, however, and came over to sit with me. For the first time in this church, and for the first time in my life, we were to wash one another's feet at evening's end, as on the night of betrayal Jesus had washed the disciples' feet. Following Lynn's guidance, I sat in a metal chair and let her kind hands strip my feet bare and lower them into the water. In my loneliness, it was a blessing simply to be touched. When we changed places, I learned as I washed her pale narrow feet that my hands were still capable of giving help and pleasure to another person. That such goodness could exist within the darkness of betrayal and death, Jesus' and mine, moved me deeply.

In the timing of the Christian year, Easter follows Maundy Thursday by only three days. But that year it did not come at all, at least not for me. On Friday, I met my friend Larry at noon, the hour at which Christians remember the death and crucifixion of Jesus. We listened as a choir sang Jesus' words from the cross, in a setting by Heinrich Schütz. *My God, my God, why have you forsaken me?* Then Larry walked with me for hours as I faced the finality of my loss. On Sunday, I dutifully went to church, but it was impossible to force an *Alleluia* from my lips.

One full year had to turn before I could rejoice and believe, in the resurrection or in much else. I moved to Providence—a good name, I thought—and waited impatiently for my story to move on to its next chapter. But my new apartment, though sunny in fact, felt like a basement. I was stuck in darkness. In October, unable to find light in the churches I visited, I decided to leave the church altogether—not just a particular church, but *the* church, all of it. I told anyone who might be interested, and when Christmas came I listened to Joni Mitchell's album *Blue* instead of to carols, wishing, with her, that I had a river I could skate away on. New Year's would provide a turning point, I hoped; but the party I attended left me feeling emptier than ever. It was a long winter.

Then came Maundy Thursday, and I could not resist the pull of the story. Around the corner from my apartment was a large church that offered a service in its stately sanctuary. I slipped into a back pew and listened, grateful to be able to blend in with the crowd, anonymous. On Friday, I went to another church to pray at noon. By Sunday, I wanted to hear the next part of the story so badly that I went again.

What I heard caught me off guard, so vivid did it seem, and so directly addressed to me. On the first day of the week, women go to the tomb with spices to honor the dead body of their teacher— women, the ones familiar with bodies, with death. But the body is gone. "Why do you seek the living among the dead?" ask two men in dazzling clothes (Luke 24:1–5). Christ had risen. No, Christ *is* risen. Hearing this good news as if for the first time, I realized that I was on the verge of being changed. I was being drawn into a story in which life prevails over death.

I knew at once that I wanted life, abundant life, but I also knew that letting go of my status as a mourner, as She Who Was Wronged, would require another little death as I relinquished a role that had become quite comfortable. I was not quite ready to allow the Easter story to shape my own. And so I turned to Nancy, who had become my friend during the past year. Nancy and her husband, Bob, lived on the edge of Narragansett Bay, in a rambling old house complete with a widow's walk. "Come stay with us," she said when I called.

As I drove out along the winding coastal road, I experienced both hope and fear, wondering if the story of resurrection I had recently heard could be trusted.

After welcoming me, Nancy let me sit alone in the sun for a little while, and then she came out of the house to sit with me on the porch. We shared a few minutes of silence in the spring sunshine, and then she suddenly turned to me, looked me full in the eyes, and said, "Your life is not over. You have a future, you know." I was not so sure, I murmured, but she kept on explaining her hope for me until it was almost evening. Then she went in to prepare supper. As she and Bob and I ate at their round oak table, I felt that I had never had a meal so nourishing. I knew in the breaking of this bread that yes, I did have a future. After supper, the three of us lingered at that table for hours, laughing and singing all our favorites from their collection of old hymnals until our voices gave out on "A Mighty Fortress Is Our God."

In the darkness of that church basement in Boston and the sunshine of Nancy's porch on Narragansett Bay, the story of my life was illumined by the life that shines from Jesus' story. The repetition of that story across the days of two years had provided points in time that opened into relationship with other people and with God. It had invited me to know myself more truthfully. It had also graced me with the assurance that I am known, not from outside time but from within it.

The embrace of the year as it is lived by Christian people at worship still enfolds me, its annual sequence of days and seasons inviting me into the gracious presence of God time after time. Because it is a year, round like any other kind of year, its seasons repeat themselves: Advent, Christmas, Epiphany, Lent, Easter, Pentecost, and then Advent once again as a new cycle begins. Within each season, specific days make manifest the mystery of God's active presence with and for the world, with and for us, as each fast or feast invites us into this mystery in a different way. At thirty, I was blessed to share the mystery of Christ on Maundy Thursday and at thirty-one to see the Risen One with the eyes of my heart. In other years, different days and seasons have been the ones to unveil the mystery and, in the unveiling, to open more doors between me and other people, between me and God.

WHAT IS THE CHRISTIAN YEAR?

More than a century ago, a French monk wrote that the liturgical year is "the joy of the people, the source of light to the learned, and the book of the humblest of the faithful." The year comprises a sequence of days and seasons, woven together in an order that tells the story of Christ and leads believers ever deeper into the mysteries of the Christian faith. It is most visible in the formal services of worship prescribed in the liturgical calendar: the services of each season, indeed of each day, draw consistently on certain biblical passages, colors, physical gestures, prayers, and music. In addition, the order of the year fosters reflection in those who join in its rhythms, as thoughts and feelings evoked in liturgy linger even after formal worship has ended. As the monk, the Benedictine scholar Prosper Guéranger, suggested, the year both delights and teaches those who enter its embrace.

Christians have celebrated liturgies that adhere to annual rhythms since the earliest days of the church. At first these rhythms were the rhythms of Judaism: Jesus celebrated Passover and other annual festivals, and so did his followers, who, like him, were Jews. Later, as Christianity spread beyond and became distinct from Judaism, its calendar became more complex and sometimes even muddled. Though building on a common story and faith, Christian communities in various regions and cultures developed calendars that were not always compatible. For most of Christian history, for example, the churches that trace their lineage to western Europe have celebrated Easter on different dates than the churches of Eastern Orthodoxy. Christianity is a still developing tradition, however, a tradition with a future as well as a past, and therefore many believers hope that someday, within history, this difference will be reconciled.

The Circling Year Draws Us into the Story of God

The Heart of the Christian Year

It is in the great reconciliation celebrated each Easter that the Christian year has its origin and finds its purpose. Here we proclaim the mystery at the center of our faith: Jesus, a human being who was completely one with God, was put to death and buried in a tomb, and on the third day he rose from the dead. This compact, dazzling story was the good news carried from person to person, from city to town, by those who experienced the presence of the risen Christ in the earliest years of the Christian movement. Jesus had passed over from life to death to life, winning a victory not only for himself but for humanity, for us. This is the story they told as they gathered for supper each week on the day that was both first and eighth, the day on which Christ's resurrection was both remembered and experienced anew, a present foretaste of a future victory. This vortex of dying and rising—Jesus' and ours in him—is the *paschal mystery*. Christians still tell it and taste it, especially when we gather for worship on Sunday.

Christ's *Pascha*—the word for the Jewish passage from bondage to freedom that Christians apply to Christ's passing from death to life—was at the center of weekly worship for the earliest Christians, although there is only the slightest hint that they observed it as an annual festival (1 Corinthians 5:7). By the end of the second century, however, some Christian communities were gathering to celebrate *Pascha* on a single night on or near the Jewish Passover. Fittingly, this night became the night on which new believers were initiated into the Christian community. In a marvelous joining of Christ's story and theirs, they too died and rose on this night; they died to sin and were raised to new life, for this was the night of their baptism. After weeks or months of preparation, the converts, known as *catechumens,* renounced the devil, confessed their faith, took off their clothing, and were anointed with oil. Then they were led into the water, all the way under, finally to emerge dripping, as naked as when they were born and just as new. In white robes, carrying lighted candles, they were led into the room where the faithful community had been fasting all night, praying for their new brothers and sisters and keeping vigil for Christ's return. They shared, for the first time, the kiss of peace; they joined, for the first time, the prayers and songs; they ate and drank, for the first time, the meal of thanksgiving. They not only heard the stories of Jesus but entered them, just as they had entered the water. Their own stories were beginning anew.

Now, as then, the specific hours during which we celebrate *Pascha* portray in crystalline form the joyous mystery into which Christians have been drawn. This is a time for worship that is daring and dramatic. As a teen, I got up very, very early on Easter mornings, while it was still dark, and went to the field behind my church. Gathered there with pastor, friends, and a few adults, I entered the story that begins, "Early on the first day of the week, while it was still dark, Mary Magdalene came to the tomb. . . ." The tomb was empty, and Mary was heartbroken, thinking that someone had stolen Jesus' body. Soon, though, she would turn and see him standing there, alive. Though she did not recognize him at first, he knew her well. "Mary!" he said to her. Then he sent her to tell the others what was happening (John 20:1–18). By the time the story had been told, the sun had risen—in that ancient graveyard and in that field behind my church. In the new light, we sang and prayed and then went inside to prepare breakfast for the other worshipers, who would soon be arriving.

For the past several years, I have celebrated *Pascha* a few hours earlier, on Easter Eve. This service, too, begins outdoors: in the darkness, a new fire is kindled, fire that will light both the candle that stands by the baptismal font symbolizing the light of Christ and the candles each worshiper will carry. In the darkness, the proclamation comes: "Christ is risen!" With candles our only light, we go into the church—often, in the bluster of springtime, it feels as if we are rushing like the wind—to settle down for a long meditation on the paschal mystery. Reading after reading tells of God's bringing light out of darkness (the creation), fruitfulness out of devastation (Noah and the flood), freedom out of bondage (the Israelites crossing the Red Sea), life out of death (Ezekiel in the valley of dry bones), safety out of peril (Shadrach, Meshach, and Abednego in the fiery furnace). Before we even get to the resurrection—right after this year's catechumens are baptized—we see that overcoming death with life is what God is always up to. The paschal mystery pervades nature and history, the Bible's time and ours.

At Easter Sunrise or Easter Vigil, on a morning in New Jersey or an evening in Indiana, Christian people gather within time, on a certain day not long after the spring equinox, to proclaim that on a similar day long ago the eternal God lived and died as a vulnerable human being, within time. And more: we proclaim that here, in time like ours, God wrestled with and overcame time's most fearsome weapon, the one we mortals know will someday end our time. And more: we proclaim that now all time is imbued with this victory. This is what I realized on that Easter Sunday evening when I was thirty-one years old: life has prevailed over death, and life still prevails over death.

I find that I need to learn this again and again, year after year. While I was still in my thirties, and they in their fifties, first Larry and then Nancy died of cancer. Their deaths were real, painful for them and for those who loved them. Afterward, however, I remember most of all how each of them helped me live more abundantly and how each also proclaimed life to many other people during the time they were given. Larry was a minister and conductor who gathered unemployed musicians into a new orchestra, raising their spirits and enhancing the shared spirit of his city. Nancy was all compassion as grandmother, teacher, and friend and also a brilliant scholar and a resolute activist whose work shed light on oppression and brought help to those whom oppression would destroy. In the often painful mingling of life and death that shaped their stories, I have no doubt that life finally had, and has, the victory.

The Full Circle of the Christian Year

In a single turning, the Christian year carries the content of Christian faith into present time, inviting us to experience the here-and-now in relation to a story that began before creation and continues into a future that is already dawning. The year encircles us with "sayings and stories, songs and prayers, processions and silences, images and visions, symbols and rituals, feasts and fasts," the Catholic theologian Mark Searle wrote, and through them all "the mysterious ways of God are not merely presented but experienced, not merely perused but lived through." Indeed, we are sometimes drawn right into these mysteries, and when we are, we do not emerge unchanged.

From *Pascha,* the heart of the year, the whole year unfolds. Historically, the other days and seasons of the liturgical year emerged over several centuries as extensions of this one festival. The season of Lent, for example, began as a period of preparation for baptism. Pentecost, which Christians celebrate as the giving of the Holy Spirit, follows Easter by fifty days, as the Jewish feast that celebrates the giving of the Law to Moses follows Passover. Christmas and Epiphany emerged in December and January because people assumed that another passing over—God becoming flesh in Mary's womb—must also have happened at *Pascha*; these feasts come nine months' gestation later. The connections among these and other festivals are not only historical, however. Each day and season of the year still echoes with the paschal mystery. Each day or season discloses in a special way the struggle of life and death in all their forms—and the ultimate victory of life.

The Christian year begins as the calendar year sputters into its final month. Its first season is quiet but expectant, leaning, as if heavy with child, into the future. During the four weeks of Advent, the season whose name means "coming," we carry our yearning in full view, like a protruding belly. Borrowing the words of the prophet Isaiah, we declare our own longing for the eyes of the blind to be opened and the ears of the deaf unstopped, and for streams of water in the desert. We dare to hope that God will indeed send good news to the oppressed and bind up the brokenhearted and repair the ruined cities (Isaiah 35:1–10, 61:1–4). Then John the Baptist, crying Isaiah's words in the wilderness, announces that God's promises are close to fulfillment. "Stir up your power and come," we pray, yearning out of the depths of history and into the promises beyond history, and out of the depths of our own lives toward the fulfillment of our deepest longings.

That fulfillment arrives in the form of a little baby. I love seeing babies at Christmas not only because they are little, like the baby Jesus, but also because they are so physical; they are all mouth and eyes and thumbs and poop, and loving them includes being close to

91

their sweet flesh. This is what God became at Christmas: human flesh, beloved and radiating love. We tell the story as the day begins in darkness on December 24: an unwed mother, the faithful man to whom she is betrothed, a bed of straw, a visit from shepherds. It happens in a stable, the place where, as the poet W. H. Auden writes, "for once in our lives / Everything became a You and nothing was an It." In our joy, we get all dressed up—this is a festival—singing carols and glowing like the candles that are everywhere on this night. On the Christmas Eve of my thirty-seventh year, a circle of glowing choir members stopped at my pew to sing "Silent Night" to me, my husband, and our newborn twins. The coming of God as a little human baby happened and happens again each year, in time and space and flesh that are palpable.

Christmas is not just one day but a season of twelve days, culminating in the feast of the Epiphany on January 6. At Epiphany— the word means an appearing, a manifestation, an "aha!"—what is happening in Jesus' story starts to become clear. We begin to see who this child is. Tradition holds that this is the day when the magi arrived to worship the child. The star that guided them is its symbol, and images of light fill Epiphany prayers and hymns. In some communities, Christmas trees whose work is done provide fuel for a great bonfire on the Eve of Epiphany; the blaze brightens the winter sky, and the sparks that fly up are accompanied by prayers for the healing of all the nations of the world, including the distant places from which the magi traveled. By the next Sunday, Jesus is all grown up, presenting himself for baptism by John, and a voice from heaven says, "You are my Son, the Beloved; with you I am well pleased" (Mark 1:11). My own son, puzzled at three to see a picture of Jesus with a beard so soon after we'd been singing "Away in a Manger," suggested that the person being baptized must be baby Jesus' daddy.

Time moves swiftly, here as elsewhere. When Christmas seems barely over, and when the light of Epiphany has only begun to disclose who Jesus is, the season of Lent arrives. The one who was a few weeks ago at a wedding, turning water into wine (John 2:1–11), now must set his face toward Jerusalem, where he will die. We are to go with him, and it is time to get ready: we have forty days to prepare, the same forty Jesus had when he went into the wilderness after his baptism, or the children of Israel when they lived only on manna, their forty days in the wilderness becoming so many years. Graciously, our wilderness days are crossed by six Sundays, which do not count in the forty and which remind us, like every Sunday all year, that we are heading not only toward death but also toward life. These Sundays are a little different from the others, even so. Their color is purple, and their songs are solemn. No one says *Alleluia;* we have put the word away, fasting from it so as to savor it more fully when Easter finally comes and so as not to forget that dying will happen before then.

Lent begins on Ash Wednesday, when we remember by the smudges on our foreheads that we are dust and to dust we shall return, and ends on Maundy Thursday, when Jesus is sentenced to death. Although it begins and ends with a cross, however, Lent's name means "spring," and its purpose is a springtime purpose. This season opens a renewing space in time, a trench into which we can shovel whatever must die in us—different for each person—before new life can come. Making good on this opportunity requires intention and attention. Like the poet-farmer Wendell Berry in "A Purification," we sort through the results of our efforts and separate the worthy from the waste. We do the earthy housekeeping of self-examination, and we confess that we have not been paying attention. Just as Jesus will soon be buried in the tomb, we bury some of what separates us from him.

> At start of spring I open a trench
> in the ground. I put into it
> the winter's accumulation of paper,
> pages I do not want to read
> again, useless words, fragments,
> errors. And I put into it
> the contents of the outhouse:
> light of the sun, growth of the ground,
> finished with one of their journeys.
> To the sky, to the wind, then,
> and to the faithful trees, I confess
> my sins: that I have not been happy

The Circling Year Draws Us into the Story of God

enough, considering my good luck;
have listened to too much noise;
have been inattentive to wonders;
have lusted after praise.
And then upon the gathered refuse
of mind and body, I close the trench,
folding shut again the dark,
the deathless earth. Beneath that seal
the old escapes into the new.

Even forty days of hard digging can scarcely prepare us for what happens next, however. For one whole week, we relive in present time a devastating sequence of events that took place in a minor city of the Roman Empire twenty centuries ago. We enter the story through dramatic liturgies that trace their roots to the fourth century, when they were developed for the throngs of pilgrims who celebrated *Pascha* at the holy places. As if we were in Jerusalem ourselves, we wave palms and shout *Hosanna!* on the day that is both Palm Sunday and Passion Sunday. The shouts soon ring hollow, however, for we know that by week's end the crowd will abandon the one we now acclaim. On Thursday, he will host us at a table of love and forgiveness, even though he knows it too.

With this meal, we enter the heart of the paschal mystery for the three days known as *Triduum*. After Thursday's arrest come Friday's crucifixion, Saturday's silence, and Sunday's glory. At last, Christ is risen, and so are we. Our words are in the present tense, and this Easter and the first one are each of them, and both together, the first day of a new creation. For the next seven weeks—Easter is a season as well as a day—those of us who usually kneel to pray will say our prayers standing up, gladly conforming our bodies to the posture of Christ. Readings, prayers, and hymns help us voice what it would mean to conform our minds and hearts as well.

For fifty days, it is Easter—more days, probably, than most of us can sustain our joy. Like the disciples after they watched the Risen One ascend on the fortieth day, we have returned to the city, to carry on with our lives (Acts 1). It is here that the gift that completes Easter finds us on the Day of Pentecost. The Holy Spirit arrives like a rushing wind, and we understand that the love and strength of God are not separate from us but now dwell in our own hearts. Our lives are meant to embody these gifts of the Spirit and to share them with others.

This is a glorious perception but also a humbling one. Those of us who kneel when we pray begin to do so again. The long season of Pentecost lies ahead; we are entering a time that the Catholic calendar calls "ordinary." We will be nourished in the paschal mystery each Sunday, and with the help of the Holy Spirit we will seek to embody its mercy in our daily living. As the months pass, however, we will become conscious again of our yearning for the advent of Christ.

LIVING IN THE STORY THROUGH THE YEAR

The story of the Christian year is a story about God's passing over into human time and about all that God has done and is still doing within this time. And it is a story that is told within time, in seasons that circle the year. Again and again, God has met me here, receiving my experience, embracing it, and giving it back to me renewed. This is what happened as I ate with Nancy and Bob on that Easter evening, which was simultaneously the evening of the disciples' supper with the risen Christ at Emmaus (Luke 24:14–35), an evening in the thirty-second year of my life, and an evening that was a foretaste of the feast to come. That evening was time to be "lived through," time so rooted in a meaningful past and so evocative of a promising future that passing through it made me more fully alive.

Sometimes the fit between my need and liturgical time is not so readily apparent. During a recent November, my family moved from one house to another. No time for Advent that year! My waiting was for carpet installers and plumbers, my palpable space a house, not a stable. Christmas came and went in a blur of household materialism, and I can barely remember Epiphany. But then came Lent. My journal includes these notes on the sermon I heard on Ash Wednesday: "Rub the sleep of death from our eyes. Get in shape. Cut the fat from around our hearts. Live simply, purely. Spend time with God." That evening at home, I scribbled out as much as I could remember. "I need Lent," I wrote; "spring, tending little shoots, clearing the soil of debris." Then I piled the catalogues and fabric swatches that had obsessed me into a trench—a box in the basement—committing them to darkness and myself to noticing the presence of God during each day of this season. My attention flagged at certain points during the next forty days, I confess, but I never retrieved the box.

The story I enter through the course of a Christian year is personal; it is spacious enough that I, with my peculiar concerns, can live through it. But it is also much more than personal. I encounter it within a worshiping community, and this community encounters it too, together. As the line of the community's shared life wends its way out of the past and into the future, the Christian year curves this line into meaningful script as well. On the Palm Sunday after the death of Martin Luther King Jr., when the *Hosannas* seemed even more ambiguous than usual and the capacity of human crowds to work death more manifest, we prayed for justice and reconciliation. During Epiphany 1991, when the light over the Middle East came not from a star but from bombs, we prayed for the innocents who were dying there, the distant cousins of the children slaughtered in that part of the world when Joseph and Mary escaped to Egypt with their newborn child (Matthew 2:16–18). Each Christmas, when we sing peaceful carols about Bethlehem, we pray for peace in the Judean countryside where shepherds once kept watch over their flocks by night.

The Christian practice of living through the year cuts against the grain of despair, as the paschal mystery at its heart touches all our stories, be they of personal or of global importance. Within the year's rhythms, there is no avoiding the presence and power of death in all its forms. This is a startling matter in itself, since often we would prefer to avoid it, and our culture is always ready to provide the means, at least for a while. But even more startling are the ways in which the year's rhythms bear life to the forefront. If we offer attention, they will teach us to listen to and live in the world differently.

The year tells a story not to be perused but to be lived through. Like the other Christian practices for opening the gift of time, however, the practice of living through the year confronts some obstacles in the contemporary context. As we pick our way through these obstacles, unsteadily at many points, we will do well to remember that this practice embodies not so much a theory of time as a set of deep convictions about what time is for. Time is for repairing ruined cities. Time is for wilderness journeys that train us for living and dying. Time is for washing feet. Time is for sharing the gifts of God's love and strength as we go about our daily work.

Though imperfectly, the lines of our lives can be curved into script that proclaims this good news.

Chapter 7

LIVING IN THE STORY THIS YEAR

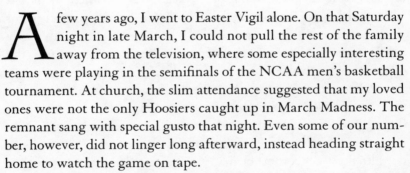

few years ago, I went to Easter Vigil alone. On that Saturday night in late March, I could not pull the rest of the family away from the television, where some especially interesting teams were playing in the semifinals of the NCAA men's basketball tournament. At church, the slim attendance suggested that my loved ones were not the only Hoosiers caught up in March Madness. The remnant sang with special gusto that night. Even some of our number, however, did not linger long afterward, instead heading straight home to watch the game on tape.

Looking back on a year, I remember the seasons from Advent to Pentecost. But I also remember many other seasons, among which the basketball season is fairly minor. I remember first semester and second semester, summer vacation, tax season, flu season. Each belongs to one of the many annual rhythms that pattern my time. I live within fiscal years, school years, and election years as well as liturgical years, and even though I find the last of these utterly alluring and nourishing, I cannot escape the others. Nor would I ever wish to escape them.

The Christian practice of living through the year encompasses not just the liturgical year but all the annual rhythms that pattern our time. The activities that shape these other years—activities like economics, education, and politics—are not distractions from the story that encircles the worshiping community. Instead, they provide the story's context and illuminate its content. Activities like these appear in every chapter of the story itself: it is full of communities and kings, teachers and disciples, crops and coins. And these activities are inside us. When we enter the mysteries of the liturgical year, we enter as people already thoroughly embedded in years of other kinds, people caught up in a complex of annual rhythms shaped by a wide range of human needs and social forces.

Christian faith and Christian liturgy treat all of these as important. Just as Advent yearning is not stuck in the long-ago time when the biblical texts associated with the season were written, so is it not restricted to the realm of the church. Advent is ours, now, and it articulates hopes that belong to all our years. At least, it is meant to do so. Often we miss it, however, its expectant voice barely perceptible amid the other sounds to which we are attuned, its muted colors hard to see in a society all covered with tinsel at this time of year. Or we do notice Advent, but only at church, isolating the story it tells from most of the stories we live. In similar ways, we miss the other seasons as well.

Discerning how to synchronize the liturgical year and the other years within which we live can be astonishingly difficult. The conflict between Easter Vigil and a basketball game provides only a tiny glimpse into a vast thicket of difficulties. I have found that my journey into this thicket must be made in the knowledge that my path is unlikely to be level and free of debris, whether in the form of basketball games or tinsel. That is all right. The Christian year does not need a broad highway. It makes its way not triumphantly, by burning a road, but gently, by pruning the underbrush that obstructs my way, at home and at work. It lops off some of the branches that block my vision of the horizon, reminding me of who I am and of what really matters. It teaches me again and again whose woods these are, something I forget all too readily.

Yet obstacles remain, obstacles much like those that clutter our days and deny us the sabbath. We are too busy to add the liturgical year to all the others whose demands we are trying to balance. Its rhythms, which perhaps we could have followed in a predominantly Christian society, don't fit in a pluralistic one. Moreover, this year simply doesn't match many of the patterns that have become most comfortable and familiar. As we have found when considering the other Christian practices for opening the gift of time, entering the Christian practice that cleaves to the span of the year will require creativity.

CAN WE ENTER THIS PRACTICE TODAY?

"When I was a girl," writes Noelle Oxenhandler, "the season of Lent had a mysterious power all its own." The power, she says, was the "power of interiority." Jesus had withdrawn into the wilderness. The statues in church were wrapped in purple cloth. Beneath the soil, bulbs were just beginning to push their shoots upward. Noelle fasted, giving up sweetened cereals one year and not speaking French another, "so as to be more ordinary." The season was delicious, its tastes enhanced because it was different from the rest of the year.

The "recurrence of difference" among seasons, weeks, and days has been "at the very core of human time" throughout history, Oxenhandler notes. As a new millennium dawns, however, temporal difference is vanishing. Instead, we live increasingly in "the twenty-four-hour time of commerce, of convenience. It is 7-Eleven time, the fluorescent time of unmodulated, shadowless light, where coffee and doughnuts are available at all hours, where the rhythm of breakfast, lunch, and dinner has no meaning, and where Sunday is Monday." Where, we might add, the only signs that holy days are near are the poinsettias on the styrofoam cups and the red and green sprinkles on the doughnuts. Where, furthermore, few hesitate before eating those doughnuts unless calories are their concern, because no one has ever suggested that they step back from habitual patterns in order to seek nourishment for the hungers within themselves.

Our society is not all fluorescence and styrofoam, at least not yet. Even so, Oxenhandler's image of time that is always the same suggests how remote the alternating patterns of both the natural year and the liturgical year have become. The wealthy can escape the seasons altogether if they wish, traveling from one clime to another all year long, ingesting in each locale the best of coffees and the finest of pastries. The middle class can have at least a January week of warmth among the talking animals in Disney's world without seasons. And in the United States, all but the very poor can eat the same food all year long. Never mind that it has to be flown in from around the world, where it is often produced at the price of justice to those who grow it.

For many Americans, a prominent recurrent difference within a year is the difference between vacation and not-vacation, between not-work and work. A week or two away compensates workers for the labors of the year past and renews them for the year ahead, or so they hope. Certain forces seem to be threatening even this respite, however. "The summer vacation, once a near-sacred ritual, is under electronic siege," announced the *New York Times* in a front-page article in July 1997. Now that technology has made it possible to work almost anywhere, people are taking their laptop computers, cellular phones, and beepers along on those precious days of not-work. Little thought has been given to limiting the use of such devices so as to enhance not only productivity but also the quality of life. Thus the demands of the business world and the personal compulsions of many high-tech workers are robbing them of even the fleeting joys of a real vacation.

Remote from the natural world and wired into a workplace that never shuts down, we are in danger of slipping into an existence that is always winter and never Christmas. My family finds renewal each summer at a retreat center located in a mountain valley so remote that it has no phone lines and so steep that cellular signals cannot be sent or received. In this is our refreshment: nature is close, and the workplace is far away. But soon, no doubt, some new satellite will "serve" even this secluded location. Those of us who love this place ask one another whether we will be able to resist the advance of technological possibility firmly enough to preserve this mountain valley as a place apart.

The trend toward structures of time that increase productivity but decrease opportunities for release, reflection, and renewal is not a force that assaults the practice of living through the year from outside the Christian community. It is one in which many of us already participate, and communities shaped by a deep commitment to liturgical time are not immune. On a recent Palm Sunday, as the members of a New York City congregation processed around the church building waving palms and singing, one of them was talking on a cellular phone. Earlier that year, as I waited inside the Church of the Holy Sepulchre in Jerusalem to enter the marble tomb revered as the place where Jesus' body lay, a cell phone rang in the pocket of the pilgrim waiting behind me. When and where in this world, I thought, can we find times and places for offering attention to God?

The answers to this question will differ for each of us, but they lie somewhere in the region where liturgy meets life. In a world where time and space within which to offer attention to God and to one another is scarce, what can we learn from the liturgical year that might guide us into years that have summers as well as winters, and festivals, and spaces fit for renewal and reflection?

GUIDANCE IN THE CHRISTIAN PRACTICE OF LIVING THROUGH THE YEAR

One morning when she was three years old, my daughter looked up from her bowl of cereal and asked an apparently simple question: "Mommy, what time is it?"

"It's morning time," I answered. Her frown instantly indicated that this was not the answer she needed. "Seven o'clock." That would not do either. "Breakfast time? Time for *Sesame Street*?" She rejected these suggestions also.

"No, no," she said, frustrated by my obtuseness. "Halloween all finished, Christmas all finished, Valentine's all finished. What *time* is it?" There was urgency in this question, an urgency even an adult could understand. If you don't know what time it is, you might miss something important: some fun, some stories, and lots of candy too.

Learning which days are important in her home, church, neighborhood, and society shapes a child profoundly. This three-year-old's short list already included an interesting assortment: one day of great meaning for her faith and two days obliquely related to the Christian calendar but now the domain of greeting card and candy companies, all three of them fun and sugary. Other special days would soon be added: her own birthday and the birthdays of others, the first day of school, and more. She caught on early that some, but not all, arose from the Christian year. A few months after the breakfast conversation, she asked if the reason for fireworks on the Fourth of July was that something was happening to Jesus again.

Because she lives in a pluralistic society, she will probably be asking similar questions—"Tell me, what is special about this day?"—all her life long. These are questions we all need to learn to ask and answer as we seek to honor the special days of our neighbors of other faiths and to share with them the meaning of our own. Indeed, they are questions that arise today even within families, when marriage creates unfamiliar combinations of this calendar and that one. The shape of the year cannot be taken for granted. Care and deliberation about this span of time are essential. When and how we measure and mark it matters immensely.

FEASTING AND FASTING

There is nothing like a special meal to mark a day as important. Certain times—Thanksgiving, Christmas, Mom's birthday—call for certain foods, and those who are in the know know which and when. Food and time can be so bound together in our memories and affections that the scent of a certain spice carries us instantly back to a certain day. Moreover, some times call not just for special food but for lots of it. When his grown children come home, a friend who is the cook in his family makes too much of everything: here are all their favorites, not one vegetable dish but three, not one bread basket but two, each overflowing with more than the family can eat. It is his love of them, not merely the food, that is running over, of course. Such occasions, whether they are on a public calendar or on days known only within a small circle, are not just meals. They are feasts. Food abounds, and so does mercy.

Two great feasts give the Christian year its shape: Christmas, the Feast of the Nativity, and Easter, the Feast of the Resurrection. Were it not for the mercy, the food served to the worshiping community at these times might seem unremarkable: bread and wine, the same meal we share every week. But mercy there is, so much that even a small amount becomes a feast when it is eaten in the company of this new baby or shared at the table of the One who has died and risen again. For most believers, these feasts overflow the cup of formal worship to resume at home. For me, an Easter feast once took place at a round table near Narragansett Bay. For my friend, the Christmas feast continues at Grandma's house, to which he, his wife, and their grown children take their too-much-food to share, along with their love.

We recognize Easter and Christmas as feasts partly because they are preceded by many days of not-feast. During Lent, a fast of forty days, we deliberately prune some of the underbrush that blocks our way to the abundant life that will be offered anew at Easter. Many people clear their palates and their minds by giving up a food that feeds desire rather than necessity or an activity that clutters life without enhancing it, such as watching television. In worship, we give up a word—*Alleluia*—and a few communities give up elaborate music, too, choosing to sing a capella during Lent. When it is time to feast again, they know it in the first booming chords of the organ.

Lent was not part of my childhood. In those years before the Second Vatican Council opened the windows on a new era of friendship between Protestant and Catholic Christianity, I would have been baffled, even offended, by Noelle Oxenhandler's enthusiasm for giving up sweetened cereals and draping the sanctuary in purple. Today, however, many Protestants are rediscovering Lent. The joy of being *synchronized,* literally "together in time," with other Christians is one reason. Another is our growing awareness that without a fast, it is hard to recognize a feast.

Come December, it seems that all the world is awash in feasting. It is the "Christmas season"—not the one that starts on December 25 but the one that opens when candy canes replace jack-o'-lanterns in the window displays at the mall. Too-much-food is evident almost everywhere: at offices, at schools, in stores. Even the shelves of food banks are full, public generosity having briefly soared. But is this really a feast? Many of us find that this season's material excesses, far from heightening our joy, can actually obstruct our pathway to the love that is its origin and purpose.

Advent, the season of expectation, prepares us to recognize the real feast when it comes and not to settle for any counterfeits, bargains or not. A feast is not just a table overflowing with food. It is a table overflowing with love as well. In early and mid-December, the heart of America's "Christmas season," many households settle in for a few minutes of quiet each day to prepare for the feast we will celebrate not now but at Christ's birth. An Advent wreath with four candles prompts our reflection: one candle is lit during the first week, two during the second, and so on. Gathered in this soft light, we redirect our yearning from things to the needs of other people and the coming of God, from material riches to the poverty of our own hearts and the poverty that afflicts the world. We remember hopes greater than those peddled at the mall.

Few families, including mine, are able to ignore the commercial din of an American "Christmas season." Many of us, however, are finding ways to listen to other sounds as well. Advent sharpens our hearing. Some churches, in a move that can be intensely controversial, sing no Christmas carols until the night of December 24. Then, and only then, comes the feast, which can stretch out to include twelve whole days that barely appear in the datebook of commerce. While others take down their trees and lights and stock up on champagne, we luxuriate in one of the most peaceful periods of the year, all the way to Epiphany on January 6 if we can manage it. Eastern Orthodox Christians see this day as the highlight of the season in any case, and it has long been a day of gift giving in communities that remember the tradition of the Three Kings. I know one Protestant family that has moved its gift exchange to this day as well, to avoid the December rush. While hardly part of a mass movement, their decision displays the kind of creativity that will be necessary if we really intend to add respite and renewal to the rhythms of a year.

Tensions between the church's time and the market's time have been tugging at Christians for many centuries, and they are likely to continue to do so. In the Middle Ages, the same festival days that brought people to the cathedrals attracted sellers to the city squares nearby, prompting church leaders even then to seek ways of protecting the church's time from the distractions of commerce. After the rise of modern business, many merchants decided, for their own reasons, that separating the two kinds of time might be a good idea after all. Ebenezer Scrooge, the miserly antihero of Charles Dickens's *Christmas Carol,* spoke for them when he snarled, "Bah, humbug!" Christmas, as he saw it, was nothing but an excuse for sloth and waste. In the years following the 1843 publication of Dickens's work, however, and partly due to its influence, the tide began to turn back. Merchants noticed that Christmas, and other holidays as well, had considerable commercial possibilities. "Never let a holiday . . . escape your attention," the *Dry Goods Chronicle* urged its readers, "provided it is capable of making your store better known or increasing the value of its merchandise." The commercial frenzy that surrounds contemporary American holidays is the fruition of this attitude, now securely established as part of the economic and cultural meaning of each year. Even Scrooge got the message. After a night of ghostly encounters, he became one of the greatest keepers of Christmas in all England, bestowing on his friends and relatives the biggest turkeys and the most lavish presents imaginable.

Festivity is hard to come by in a society that sets its sights intently on productivity. Therefore, it is not an entirely bad thing when commerce lends energy and publicity to our festivals, argues a thoughtful historian who has studied the buying and selling of American holidays; after all, don't human beings need periodic revelry and extravagance? The historian makes a point worth considering. Being utterly rational about the gifts we buy and ever vigilant lest we lapse into extravagance is reminiscent of the unreformed Scrooge and not fully in keeping with either our human need to feast or God's apparent intention that we do so. And yet what kind of feast is accompanied by no fast, no self-examination, and little attention to the needs of others?

The recurrence of different kinds of time through the seasons of the Christian year situates the celebration of Christmas, Easter, and other days of gladness within a rhythm as sustaining as the rhythm of breathing: our lungs fill and release, fill and release. Living through the Christian year, we enter a story rich in both food and love. We experience waiting as well as fulfillment, doing without as well as abundance. A year is a long time, and we have to wait for its story to move from one chapter to another. But when, finally, it is time to sing "Joy to the World" or to welcome grown children home or to break bread at a round table by the bay, we may taste a joy that cannot be bought. Such times are all gift.

RITUAL AND RITUALISM, REGULARITY AND ROTE

I grew up in a Christian community that had long distrusted both fasts and feasts. The seasonal round evident in most churches, and indeed in most religious communities of any sort, was only dimly visible in mine. We Presbyterians had inherited a style of plain and simple worship from our Reformed forebears, who had forged their identity in opposition to the elaborate liturgical forms of the Church of Rome and the Church of England during the Reformations of the sixteenth and seventeenth centuries. To them, as to many other Protestants since then, the liturgical year seemed to be a distraction from the straightforward message of salvation preached by the apostles.

Seasons not specifically mentioned in the Bible—Lent, for example—were of "merely human origin." In 1522, the Swiss reformer Ulrich Zwingli signaled his break with Roman Catholicism by eating sausages during Lent, rebelling against the tradition of fasting from meat during that season. A century later, the leaders of the tiny band of Protestants at Plymouth colony in New England required anyone who insisted on celebrating Christmas to do so behind closed doors. The date of Jesus' birth, they reasoned, is not established in scripture.

In their view, the sabbath provided a complete, and completely biblical, architecture of sacred time. They observed it resolutely.

Protestant dissenters from the liturgical calendar were often motivated by a desire to restore worship to the forms they believed prevailed in the early church. Beyond this, they also delivered to their contemporaries—and can still deliver to us—an important critique that is surely as old as liturgy itself, and just as biblically grounded. "I hate, I despise your festivals, and I take no delight in your solemn assemblies," God declared through the prophet Amos; "take away from me the noise of your songs." What God desired instead was justice that rolled down like waters and "righteousness like an everflowing stream" (Amos 5:21–24). When feasting and fasting turn in on themselves, those who engage in them have not entered the story of God at all; they are doing something else. When feasting and fasting are detached from life because they are too lavish or insincere or self-congratulatory, they bear bad fruit, not good. An alternative, then, is to simplify, to keep sabbath, and to seek justice and righteousness.

Groups who are wary of liturgical seasons, whether they reject them altogether or simply mute their tones and colors, give voice to a crucial point. It is possible for ritual to become rote, for vivid displays to become distractions, and for regular rhythms to lull even well-intentioned worshipers into complacency. Even the Orthodox theologian Alexander Schmemann, a great lover of the liturgy, warned that without the unsettling presence of the Holy Spirit, the liturgical year can become "the more or less antiquated decoration of religion," a quaint "audio-visual aid" instead of a "root of Christian life and action." It is possible to participate in one liturgy after another and experience only vanity. The seasons become a root of Christian life and action only when they draw us into the story of God, implicating us in the future of peace and healing that is already breaking into the present time. Occasionally, though, the Christian year can draw us in without our realizing it. I sometimes sit in church, bored and distracted, thinking that vanity is indeed my reward, only to discover hours or months later that the story has been working on me all along. The seasons can root us even when we are not completely attentive to them.

Because we are finite, we need regularity. Also because we are finite, however, we too readily convert regularity into the rigidity of unexamined custom. This happens both in worshiping communities and in communities of other sorts, especially when behavior has taken on the repetitive, symbolic character of ritual. The critical eye of the dissenter speaks an important word regarding not only ecclesiastical liturgies but other activities as well. Sports, for example, are full of rituals; in fact, ball games and religious assemblies are probably the two main places in which large numbers of people sing together, chant together, and yearn together toward a desired future. Schools of all kinds sustain rituals, too, especially when classes begin and end each year. Alertness to the possibly stifling hold of unexamined custom in activities like these can prompt questions akin to those of liturgical dissenters. When do these rituals become too lavish or insincere or self-congratulatory? Do the forms of competition they foster bear bad fruit or good?

Watchful communities will examine their annual customs every now and then, asking what stories they tell. At the retreat center I have mentioned, for example, July 25 used to be celebrated as "Christmas in July." It was kind of goofy, kind of fun: for one day, lampposts were wrapped like candy canes, ornamental sugar cookies were baked and shared, and carols poured from speakers in the street. After a couple of decades, however, the merriness wore thin. Some people said the festival died because the idea had been intrinsically tiresome all along, while others were glad to see it go because they thought that the Nordic imagery of the event excluded many people. Everyone agreed, however, that having a festival at a high point in the summer was important. And so "Summer Jubilee" came into being. Its inspiration was the biblical concept of the jubilee year, the fiftieth year, in which the ancient Israelites were enjoined to forgive debts, restore land, and reconcile with one another (Leviticus 25). On this day, the fiftieth of this community's summer season, people now work together on a land reclamation project, write letters asking for or offering forgiveness, and raise funds on behalf of an economically needy community elsewhere. They also have a big party.

Creativity of this sort resists rigidity, rounding out the year in a way that speaks memory and hope to this particular community.

On a much larger scale, the holiday of Kwanzaa, celebrated at the end of the calendar year in many African American homes, displays a creative reshaping of time as well. Either one of these young holidays has the capacity to become rigid in its time, of course, but for the time being they seem to be bearing good fruit.

REPETITION

Because years are round, each year revisits dates we have met before. Some of the dates are almost anonymous, but others wear familiar faces. A woman who has lost her spouse traces his memory through the calendar: his birthday, when they met, when they married, when they first learned that he was ill, when he entered the hospital, when he died. The intensity may diminish as one year follows the next, but these dates will always bear his image. Similarly, the date of a triumph—a personal success or one belonging to a whole nation—resonates year after year.

Repetition gives the present year its wholeness. But it is also repetition that provides vantage points from which to see beyond the present year, affording the specific footholds in time from which we look back and peer forward. Recurring dates are like the pencil marks on the woodwork that record how much a child has grown from one birthday to the next. Moving through the years, we change, returning to each anniversary or holiday a little taller (or, later, shorter) than before. One more year has passed, and we are one year farther away from our birth. How many years this makes altogether is a sum of which we keep very close track indeed.

The annual occasion on which the sum increases by one provides an obvious opportunity for looking back and peering forward. As a child, I always felt like the center of attention on my birthday, whether I was or not. Now, frankly, it can feel a little odd that this day is not, to outward appearance, so different from the others after all. Even so, heightened sensitivity to my memories, my hopes, and my inner struggles arises without my consciously seeking it. Thus I am beginning to wonder whether I should set aside some time on this day, alone and with others, to reflect on the gift of time that I have received. What would this look like for an adult? Different, I think, from the gallows humor of the over-the-hill parties that seem to be popular among other aging baby boomers.

Some other dates, perhaps dates that we carry around in the secret places of our hearts, also cry out for reflection at each annual return. The anniversaries of grave loss or injury, for example, can swamp us with renewed feelings of vulnerability. A few of those who have survived violent crime begin to tremble, in spite of themselves, as the day of their violation draws near. Caring companions do well to offer attention to this trembling.

One way to do this is deliberately to cultivate other anniversaries that impart strength, reclaiming time as a gift even in painful situations. Christian communities have been doing just this for many centuries. Apart from the celebration of *Pascha,* the setting aside of certain dates for the commemoration of saints provides the church's oldest annual rhythm. In the early centuries, most of those so honored were martyrs who lost their lives to Roman persecution. One of these, Polycarp, the beloved bishop of Smyrna in Asia Minor, was burned at the stake around the year 155. After he died, his Christian friends put his bones in a suitable place. "There the Lord will permit us, so far as possible, to gather together in joy and gladness to celebrate the day of his martyrdom as a birthday," a follower wrote. The community of believers who survived him found strength in the positive example of this sainted one, knowing that they too might ultimately face death at the hands of the empire. Similar acts of devotion, over the centuries, gave rise to a sanctoral calendar that named hundreds of saints. Among these, just one was likely to be especially dear to a given believer.

Finding inspiration in the memory of "sainted" ones continues to be a source of inspiration and strength, though the sanctoral calendar itself has been the subject of frequent disputes and reforms over the years. The Catholic church conducted a major revision in 1969, removing the names of those whose stature was sheerly local or even legendary; new names continue to be added, but only after careful consideration. As for Protestants, we have always been wary of venerating individual saints. But we do it anyway. A powerful example comes from the French village of Le Chambon, where inhabitants processed each year, singing, to a site commemorating the faithful deaths of their Huguenot forebears, who were martyred for refusing to abjure their Protestant beliefs. This memory of resolution in the face of oppression was etched into the character of these villagers, who are now, themselves, remembered for their courageous hospitality to thousands of Jews fleeing Nazi persecution during the Second World War.

Certain days call to mind and heart the sainted people of our own lives. The ones we honor in the present will form the imagination with which we approach the future. In communities, in households, and in our individual hearts, therefore, we need to discern which to honor, year after year. What are the days that can build us up in memory and hope? Often these are days touched by paschal mystery, days marked by death that ultimately become celebrations of life. In Central America and among North Americans involved in El Salvador's long struggle for justice, for example, some whose lives were cut short are remembered on the dates of their deaths: Maura Clarke, Ita Ford, Dorothy Kazel, and Jean Donovan on December 2, Bishop Oscar Romero on March 24. In the United States, the birthday of Dr. Martin Luther King Jr. on January 15 provides an annual occasion for both recollecting his martyrdom and renewing his ideals. Such days exist on a personal level, too, known only to the ones that hold them dear. Mother's Day has become more special to me in recent years, ever since my grandmother died on the following day. I remember our last conversation—I am still grateful that I called her that Mother's Day—and I remember her.

SUMMER AND WINTER, SUNDAY AND MONDAY, EVENING AND MORNING

As a single year circles around the line that is a life, it brings many occasions for reflection, remembrance, and renewal. Each community or household can gain strength from offering attention to these gifted pieces of time. Part of the challenge is to discern which days hold these gifts for each of us.

Every year on the first Sunday of Advent, my husband and children and I celebrate the anniversary of the children's baptism. We get out the white candles they were given at the baptismal font and set them on the dinner table. While the children are growing taller, we notice, these candles are getting a little shorter each year. We light them, and we also light the first candle on the Advent wreath. Our usual table prayer, "Come, Lord Jesus, be our guest, and let these gifts to us be blest," suddenly seems especially appropriate, for now we are in the season that means "coming." In the soft light, we share a special meal and reminisce. "You were so tiny," we tell the children, "and we felt so blessed; we still feel so blessed."

Then we go into the family room to sing. Accompanied by a tape, the four of us sing the vespers service written for the retreat center we visit each summer. *Jesus Christ, you are the light of the world, the light no darkness can overcome,* we begin. When we sang these words in the summer, it was still light outside after supper, but now it is December and dark. *Stay with us now for it is evening, and the day is almost over,* we continue. These words from Luke's story of Easter evening are the words I once heard from my friend Nancy. The future she saw for me is now. *Let your light scatter the darkness, and shine within your people here.* A hymn follows, and prayers; throughout, we four are reminded that we are God's people.

On this sabbath night we receive time—summer and winter, morning and evening—as the gift of God. And in this gifted time, we know one another as God's gifts as well. The next morning, off we will go to school and to work, to doctors' appointments and music lessons and committee meetings that may run well into the evening. Our lives are complicated; one year another engagement even led us to skip this little celebration, something I hope won't happen again. An annual evening like this one doesn't resolve all our conflicts regarding time by any means. In fact, on this evening, of all evenings, I perceive with clarity that all our time—not just this week's time—is limited. The shortness of the candles and the height of the children allow for no other conclusion. And yet, amid all these gifts, this doesn't seem to matter. I am strengthened to receive the day that began at sundown, the day that will soon be another challenging Monday, as God's gift as well.

Chapter 8

LEARNING TO COUNT OUR DAYS

L arry, the friend who walked with me on Good Friday when I was thirty years old, died when he was only fifty-two. His death came on Saint Valentine's Day, a day that seemed appropriate to those who knew him well. At his memorial service, a young woman who was Larry's colleague told of another day in February, a little over a year before. She was crying in the office they shared, and when he expressed concern, she told him she had just broken up with her boyfriend. Larry responded by putting his arm around her and asking, "Will you be my groundhog?" He was one who led from the heart.

When Larry's colleague told this story, she led the gathered congregation in remembering their husband, father, son, and friend. He was remembered—put back together—through her words, through the words of others who knew him and the words of liturgy, and through music and mutual embraces. On a certain afternoon in a certain year, a certain community, gathered just this once for just this purpose, remembered one particular man. He whose personhood had been shadowed by disease for several months was restored to health in their imagination. Each one could see the twinkle in his eye as he asked his young colleague this question. He took his place among them again, now not as flesh but as memory.

When death comes, we whose lives have a little longer to run do what we can to remember the days, weeks, and years whose total is a single human life. This is the span of time that is the most precious to us of all—and the most puzzling. Its duration seems so arbitrary, so unrhythmic in comparison to the regularities of the other spans of time within which we live. Why do some people live to a ripe old age, while others receive less of this precious life-time, this time given for life? We want to know, but we don't.

What we do know is who—Larry, this time. And so we remember. We hold the person in our hearts, and we name the person again as a child of God, as he or she was named at baptism. In many churches, we place over the coffin a white cloth like the cloth that wraps the newly baptized, and we light the same candle that illuminates the baptismal font. We remember, even if through tears and doubts, that in baptism this person had already died the only death that matters. And we remember the story of Jesus' own death, a story that leads beyond death. As we enter this story and yield our dear one to its movements, the remembering, the putting back together, becomes not ours but God's.

THE QUALITY OF TIME

Whenever death comes near, I am prompted to ponder my own death, and thus my life. What is the measure of my days, weeks, and years, those I have had so far and those that remain? All of us wonder, naturally, about the quantity of this measure. More important, however, is its quality. Are we living lives that are good, in some large sense? Lives that contribute to the well-being of other people, close at hand and far away, and to our own well-being? Lives that are attuned to the good of creation and to the active presence of God?

When our lives are perpetually out of sync, when time is more problem than gift, we are necessarily unsatisfied with our answers to these questions. The quality of our lives is deeply entwined with the shape of our days, weeks, and years. When acquaintances become friends, the mutual gift of time is a necessary ingredient. Brothers and sisters, nieces and nephews, parents and children—all are related by blood, but they become family only when time is shared. The same is true in our work: without time, no bandage will be on the wound, no supper on the table, no roof on the building. Time in itself is not enough, but when time is absent, nothing else is present.

A life that is not well lived in time can be the source of immense grief. To squander one's life-time is tragic. A saying distills this wisdom: "No one ever cried out on his deathbed, 'God, I wish I had spent more time at the office!'" I am not so sure this is accurate: leaving an important project unfinished, a piece of work that represents one's contribution to human well-being, can indeed be a source of great anguish, for integrity in time takes many forms. But the saying's larger point is valid nonetheless. The desperate hyperactivity entailed in perpetually spending "more time at the office," whatever one's "office" may be, has blighted the quality of many lives, and a deathbed view of one's whole life can make this plain. The saying cautions those of us not yet on our deathbeds to give our time where it matters most.

"The most precious thing a human being has to give is time," says a woman whose lifework has been to offer hospitality to students and young adults at points of transition in their lives. Her work requires an especially generous offering of time. It is clear that even hospitality on a more modest scale cannot exist, however, if people do not open time in their lives for others. In an era when many of us feel that time is our scarcest resource, hospitality falters. If we are most comfortable when doing several things at once, does this not diminish our capacity to be still and to offer attention to a stranger or a friend? "In a fast-food culture," a wise Benedictine monk observes, "you have to remind yourself that some things cannot be done quickly. Hospitality takes time." And so do all the other practices that are fundamental to the well-being of humanity and all creation.

Hospitality and other crucial practices take time. When they take all of our time, however, they become destructive, to ourselves and often to others as well. Day after day of welcoming strangers, with no sabbath rest, drives hospitality and its practitioners to distraction; their welcome becomes unwelcoming. Indeed, even a few hours of care for the most needy strangers can do this if the host forgets that she is finite and able to do today only what she can do today. The practice of hospitality and the practices of receiving the day, keeping sabbath, and living through the year depend on one another for their fullest embodiments.

Christian practices for opening the gift of time provide one point of entry into an entire way of life. In exploring practices dealing with time, accordingly, we have encountered other Christian practices at every turn. How can we receive the day as a gift if we enter it enslaved to the past and fearful of the future—that is, if we enter it without the practice of forgiveness? Likewise, the day can withhold its blessings if we fail to remember that each day of living also involves us in the practice of dying well. As for the sabbath, it is imbued with the practices of honoring the body, singing our lives to God, household economics, and more. "The sabbath cannot survive in exile, a lonely stranger among days of profanity," Abraham Heschel declared, teaching a point that sabbath's implications for the practices that involve us all week long makes plain again and again. "The sabbath needs the companionship of all the other days." To comprehend the relationship between sabbath keeping and gratitude for creation, for example, is to take a first step into the practice of caring for the well-being of the planetary household we share, a practice that needs our participation every day. Of course, the step could just as well come from the other direction, if love for the earth prompted someone to consider keeping sabbath. When I entered the story of the Christian year, I found healing first and a way of understanding the shape of time only after years of practice. Busy people who enter these practices seeking the gift of time may end up finding that they are being healed, perhaps of ills they did not even know they had. This way of life is full of gifts. Time is only one of them.

QUANTITIES OF TIME

Even within this gifted way of life, many aspects of the problem of time will remain, simply because the structures that sustain them are so pervasive. It is likely that the boundaries between day and night, Sunday and Monday, summer and winter, will continue to blur and that the clock will keep hurrying us along, too rigidly and too fast. Even so, when Christian practices have helped us notice time that has quality, we become less vulnerable to time that does not. Growing into habits and dispositions of freedom under God, we become better able to resist patterns that are malign. If we find ourselves in Lilliput, surrounded by tiny people, they will not wonder whether our watch is our god, and neither will we.

Understanding time as God's gift will make us more, rather than less, dissatisfied with the way in which economic, social, and cultural forces structure time, thereby impelling us to become partners with others in changing unjust structures of time. In *The Time Bind: When Work Becomes Home and Home Becomes Work,* Arlie Russell Hochschild calls for a "time movement," an organized effort to develop economic structures that permit both adults and children to move more humanely within time. The emergence of such a movement will depend on people who have a substantive vision of time that has quality and who possess a certain independence from the anxious pursuit of ever more wealth, status, and security. Christian practices for opening the gift of time provide a path to such visionary independence. Those who enter these Christian practices should ally themselves with others who also yearn for greater justice and freedom in society's structures of time.

For the time being, entering the Christian practices explored in this book can make a difference in the quality of our time, even within a structurally unsupportive society. These are not practices that anyone can sustain all by oneself, however. We receive this day and keep sabbath and live through the year not alone but with *companions,* literally, "those with whom we share bread." As we have seen, it is never easy to discern what form keeping sabbath or any other practice might take in a particular complicated situation; but it is easier when we share this discernment with others and when we share some of sabbath's freedom with them as well. Small steps may be all that can be imagined or afforded at first, but that is alright. Start where you can, and let the practice begin to work in you and on you. It may lead you farther than you could have planned.

Time will continue to be messy, but it can be messy and a gift at the same time.

THE GIFTS OF TIME

I did not go to Larry's funeral or to Nancy's. One trip was canceled because of a sick child, and the other was never scheduled because my husband was out of town that week. My absence on those days was a great disappointment to me, though probably not to anyone else. I manage to disappoint others in different ways: scarcely a day passes that I do not find I have had too little time to attend to someone as I should. Living in time does not seem to be something I will ever get quite right. Practice does not make perfect.

We imperfect ones find companions and help in the Psalter, the book that Dietrich Bonhoeffer commended to his seminarians as the prayer book of the church and the prayer book of Jesus. One psalm, the ninetieth, is called in ancient texts "A Prayer of Moses, the Man of God." Tradition holds that Moses spoke these words on Mount Pisgah, the mountain at the edge of the wilderness from which he and the tribes of Israel could at last look down into the promised land (Deuteronomy 34). After forty years of practicing life as a free people under the law—living on manna, learning to trust that they would find enough food each morning, learning not to work on the sabbath—they had reached their destination. But Moses was dying. He would never enter the land he was now seeing for the first time. Like all of us, whatever our work, he had to trust future generations to complete it. It did not matter that he was a greater mortal than any other, one "whom the Lord knew face to face." He was mortal nonetheless. He ran out of time.

This psalm sets the human life span on the grandest stage imaginable. Our time—*seventy years, or perhaps eighty, if we are strong*—is played out on a temporal stage that runs *from everlasting to everlasting.* This stage belongs to the One for whom a thousand years is *like yesterday when it is past, or like a watch in the night.* Time so vast seems impervious to our brief existence, or even hostile: we are *dust,* and the years of our lives are *dream,* or *grass,* or *sigh.* The contrast could not be sharper.

And yet the psalm brings these two kinds of time—our short sigh and God's mountainous eternity—together. At the psalm's center are *our days,* particular days, days that are of a finite and finally knowable quantity, like the actual days we pass from birth to death. *So teach us to count our days,* the psalmist prays, *that we might gain a wise heart.*

This psalm, which strips us of all delusions about our duration and durability, begins nonetheless in confidence. *Lord, you have been our dwelling place in all generations.* This psalm is not a cry of cosmic homelessness but an appeal that arises from within a dwelling place more enduring than the mountains, more ancient than the world itself. And in the last five verses, the psalmist makes bold to implore this *Lord,* now identified even more confidently as *the Lord our God.* The psalmist petitions God for everything that constitutes a good, even though finite, human life: God's love each morning, enough days of gladness to balance the days of affliction, the capacity to notice God's power and to show it to our children, and such divine favor as would *prosper the work of our hands!* These petitions do not express a desire to unseat God or to live forever. Instead, they articulate a down-to-earth yearning for middling happiness, faithful children, and bountiful harvests.

Only a dwelling place of the breadth and depth of God can finally count and hold all the days, weeks, and years of humankind. And it is only within this dwelling place that we mortals can ever count our days wisely. To count is to attend to each piece one by one, knowing its true value and acknowledging that the sum will not be infinite. Counting, in this sense, helps us know the true value of a day and attend to the gifts each one bears—just what the practices that guide us in receiving time as a gift of God would have us do.

I began this exploration of Christian practices regarding time because I so yearned for more, and better, time. I wanted to be able to answer well when someone asked, "How was your day?" I wanted to find justification for not grading papers every single day of the week. I wanted to be part of a story where it is neither always winter and never Christmas nor always Christmas and never winter. What I found was that I have been exploring these practices all my life, beginning nearly fifty years ago. My parents fed and bathed me and then taught me to do these things for myself; they presented me for baptism and taught me bedtime prayers. The exploration continued as I learned a weekly rhythm of work and rest, abandoned it, and then found it again, this time with less certainty and greater improvisation than before, but also with greater need. The exploration formed me year after year, when as a teenager I got up while it was still dark on Easter mornings, and when years later I ate with Nancy and Bob on an Easter night, and when this year I warmed myself by a new fire on Easter Eve.

When we enter practices like these, we do not so much open the gift of time as find that the gift of time has been opened for us. And what we receive, we discover, is not only this gift but all the other gifts time bears as well.

References

PREFACE

"Time Talks" is from Edward T. Hall, *The Silent Language* (New York: Doubleday, 1959). *The Time Trap* is by Alec Mackenzie (New York: American Management Association, 1990); *Timelock* is by Ralph Keyes (New York: HarperCollins, 1991); and *The Time Bind: When Work Becomes Home and Home Becomes Work* is by Arlie Russell Hochschild (New York: Henry Holt, 1997). "What is time?" is from *The Confessions of Saint Augustine,* trans. Henry Chadwick (New York: Oxford University Press, 1992), p. 230.

CHAPTER ONE

Books that analyze time from a social scientific perspective include Hochschild, *The Time Bind;* Eviatar Zerubavel, *Hidden Rhythms: Schedules and Calendars in Social Life* (Chicago: University of Chicago

Press, 1981); Juliet B. Schor, *The Overworked American: The Unexpected Decline of Leisure* (New York: Basic Books, 1992); Gary Cross, *Time and Money: The Making of Consumer Culture* (London: Routledge, 1993); Edward T. Hall, *The Dance of Life: The Other Dimension of Time* (New York: Doubleday, 1983); and Jeremy Rifkin, *Time Wars: The Primary Conflict in Human History* (New York: Vintage Books, 1992). The story about Robert Maxwell and quotations from Jenny Shaw are from "Punctuality and the Everyday Ethics of Time," *Time and Society,* 1994, *3,* 79–97. On cultural differences, see Robert Levine, *A Geography of Time* (New York: Basic Books, 1997), pp. xiii–xvi. The corporate study mentioned in connection with community is Hochschild's *Time Bind.* Isaac Watts, "O God, Our Help in Ages Past," appears in many hymnals, including the *Lutheran Book of Worship* (Minneapolis: Augsburg Fortress, 1978), hymn 320. *Babette's Feast* is a Danish film directed by Gabriel Axel (1987), based on a short story by Isak Dinesen.

CHAPTER TWO

Philip Larkin's poem "Days" is in his *Collected Poems* (London: Marvel Press, 1989), p. 67. Eugene H. Peterson develops a biblical account of the day in *Working the Angles: The Shape of Pastoral Integrity* (Grand Rapids, Mich.: Eerdmans, 1987), p. 69. The testimony quoted in connection with the practice of receiving the day is from Thomas Hoyt Jr., "Testimony," in *Practicing Our Faith: A Way of Life for a Searching People,* ed. Dorothy C. Bass (San Francisco: Jossey-Bass, 1997), p. 94. Martin E. Marty tells of his daily practice in *How I Pray,* ed. Jim Castelli (New York: Ballantine Books, 1994), p. 89; the quotation from Martin Luther's *Large Catechism* is from *The Book of Concord,* trans. and ed. Theodore G. Tappert (Minneapolis: Augsburg Fortress, 1959), p. 446. Dietrich Bonhoeffer wrote of the shape of the day at Finkenwalde in *Life Together* (Minneapolis: Augsburg Fortress, 1996), pp. 48–92; quotations from pp. 55, 68, 75, 91, 92. On the liturgical hours of prayer, see Robert Taft, *The Liturgy of the Hours in East and West: The Origins of the Divine Office and Its Meaning for Today* (Collegeville, Minn.: Liturgical Press, 1993).

On the history of the clock, see Lewis Mumford, *Technics and Civilization* (Orlando: Harcourt Brace, 1934), pp. 12–18; Michael O'Malley, *Keeping Watch: A History of American Time* (Washington, D.C.: Smithsonian Institution Press, 1990); and Gerhard Dohrn–van Rossum, *History of the Hour* (Chicago: University of Chicago Press, 1996). The Lilliputian remark is from Jonathan Swift, *Gulliver's Travels* (New York: Norton, 1961; originally published in 1727), p. 18. The Hochschild quotation is from *The Time Bind,* p. 215. Statistics on employment are from Carol Kleiman, "Odd Hours: Moving to an Around-the-Clock Economy," *Chicago Tribune,* Jan. 28, 1996.

CHAPTER THREE

Kathleen Norris, *The Quotidian Mysteries: Laundry, Liturgy, and "Women's Work"* (New York: Paulist Press, 1998), pp. 40–42. Regarding the monks' schedules, see *The Rule of St. Benedict,* ed. Timothy Fry, O.S.B. (Collegeville, Minn: Liturgical Press, 1981), p. 203 (RB 8.1–4). On napping, see Martin E. Marty, "How I Relax," in *Coping in the '80s: Eliminating Needless Stress and Guilt,* ed. Joel Wells (Chicago: Thomas More Press, 1986), pp. 105–108.

"Five A.M. in the Pinewoods" appears in Mary Oliver, *House of Light* (Boston: Beacon Press, 1990), pp. 32–33. The quotation from Annie Dillard is from *Pilgrim at Tinker Creek* (New York: Harper-Collins, 1974), p. 82. Simone Weil, "Reflections on the Right Use of School Studies with a View to the Love of God," is in *Waiting for God* (New York: Putnam, 1951). The story about Roberta Bondi is in her book *In Ordinary Time: Healing the Wounds of the Heart* (Nashville, Tenn.: Abingdon Press, 1996), pp. 48–49.

On television viewing, see Robert D. Putnam's foreword to John P. Robinson and Geoffrey Godbey, *Time for Life: The Surprising Ways Americans Use Their Time* (University Park: Pennsylvania State University Press, 1997), p. xvii. Henri J. M. Nouwen writes on interruptions in *Reaching Out* (New York: Doubleday, 1975), pp. 36–37. Jane Kenyon's "Otherwise" is from *Otherwise: New and Selected Poems* (St. Paul, Minn.: Graywolf Press, 1996), p. 214. The information on Kenyon's illness is from Donald Hall's "Afterword" to this book, p. 218.

The prayer quoted in connection with compline is the opening sentence from the *Lutheran Book of Worship*'s compline service, which it calls "Prayer at the Close of the Day," p. 154. A wonderful and practical little book on compline and the larger meaning of night in the Christian practice of receiving the day is Melissa Musick Nussbaum, *I Will Lie Down This Night* (Chicago: Liturgy Training Publications, 1995); its morningtime companion book is *I Will Rise Up This Day*. Thanks to Susan Briehl for the insight about bedtime, which she develops in *Practicing Our Faith: A Guide for Conversation, Learning, and Growth* (San Francisco: Jossey-Bass, 1997), p. 46.

CHAPTER FOUR

See Karl Barth, *Church Dogmatics,* vol. 3 (Edinburgh: Clark, 1958), pp. 213 ff., and Jürgen Moltmann, *God in Creation* (Minneapolis: Augsburg Fortress, 1993), p. 276. The observations attributed to Abraham Joshua Heschel are from *The Sabbath: Its Meaning for Modern Man* (New York: Farrar, Straus & Giroux, 1952), pp. 28–29. Heschel's book has been an important source in recent Jewish and Christian reflection on the importance of the sabbath. Other important sources are Samuel H. Dresner, *The Sabbath* (New York: Burning Bush Press, 1970), and Irving Greenberg, *The Jewish Way* (New York: Touchstone, 1988). On historical developments, see *The Sabbath in Jewish and Christian Traditions,* eds. Tamara C. Eskenazi, Daniel J. Harrington, and William H. Shea (New York: Crossroad, 1991). On the relationship between these two traditions and their observance of sabbath, see Mary C. Boys, *Has God Only One Covenant?* (Mahwah, N.J.: Paulist Press, 2000).

On social conditions that challenge the practice of keeping sabbath, see Schor, *The Overworked American;* the quotation is from p. xv.

CHAPTER FIVE

Regarding time and consumerism, working and spending: several years after publishing *The Overworked American,* Juliet B. Schor turned to a related subject in *The Overspent American: Upscaling, Downshifting, and the New Consumer* (New York: Basic Books, 1998).

Heschel's story about worry is from *The Sabbath,* p. 32. Jürgen Moltmann makes his suggestions about cars in *God in Creation,* p. 296. The poem "Obedience" is from Sietze Buning (Stanley Wiersma), *Purpaleanie and Other Permutations* (Orange City, Ia.: Middleburg Press, 1978), pp. 53–54. On "event time," see Levine, *Geography of Time,* pp. 81–100. The story about the rest home workers is from my friend Maggie Fink's response to *Practicing Our Faith.* Eugene Peterson's account of a pastor's Monday sabbath is in his *Working the Angles,* pp. 63–83.

On sports, see Nichole M. Christian, "Parents Object to Cardinal's Comments over Playing Little League Games on Sundays," *New York Times,* May 18, 1998, and Tiffany Vail, "Churches Unite to Reclaim Sunday for Family Worship," *United Church News,* June 1998. On Calvin and bowling, James H. Nichols, *The History and Character of Calvinism* (New York: Oxford University Press, 1954), p. 233. The theological suggestions regarding Saturday and Monday are in Moltmann, *God in Creation,* pp. 295–296, and Alexander Schmemann, *For the Life of the World* (Crestwood, N.Y.: St. Vladimir's Seminary Press, 1995; originally published in 1963), p. 51.

Two helpful books on keeping sabbath are Marva J. Dawn, *Keeping the Sabbath Wholly* (Grand Rapids, Mich.: Eerdmans, 1989), and Tilden Edwards, *Sabbath Time* (New York: Seabury Press, 1982).

CHAPTER SIX

The Lion, the Witch, and the Wardrobe (first published in 1950) is the first volume of C. S. Lewis's *Chronicles of Narnia.* The song about the seasons as a carousel is "The Circle Game," from Joni Mitchell's 1970 album *Ladies of the Canyon* (Reprise 6376).

My telling of the story of Jesus' last supper incorporates elements from the Gospels of Matthew, Mark, and Luke. In John's Gospel, Jesus washes Peter's feet. Typically, only one of these accounts would be read in an actual Maundy Thursday service, as was surely the case in this church. The sad song in my story is "River," from Joni Mitchell's 1971 album *Blue* (Reprise 2038).

The observations attributed to Abbot Prosper Guéranger, O.S.B., are from *The Liturgical Year, I: Advent,* trans. Dom Laurence Shepherd, O.S.B. (Powers Lake, N.D.: Marian House, 1983), pp. 11–12, 16–17. Other works on the liturgical year that have informed my interpretations are Frank C. Senn, *Christian Liturgy: Catholic and Evangelical* (Minneapolis: Augsburg Fortress, 1997); Gordon Lathrop, *Holy Things: A Liturgical Theology* (Minneapolis: Augsburg Fortress, 1993); James F. White, *Introduction to Christian Worship* (Nashville, Tenn.: Abingdon Press, 1990); James F. White, *A Brief History of Christian Worship* (Nashville, Tenn.: Abingdon Press, 1993); Cheslyn Jones, Geoffrey Wainwright, Edward Yarnold, S.J., and Paul Bradshaw, eds., *The Study of Liturgy* (New York: Oxford University Press, 1992); Thomas Merton, *Seasons of Celebration* (New York: Farrar, Straus & Giroux, 1965); and Thomas J. Talley, *The Origins of the Liturgical Year* (New York: Pueblo, 1991).

The quotation from Mark Searle is from "Sunday: The Heart of the Liturgical Year," in *The Church Gives Thanks and Remembers,* ed. Lawrence Johnson (Collegeville, Minn.: Liturgical Press, 1974), p. 13. The lines by W. H. Auden are from "For the Time Being: A Christmas Oratorio" in *W.H. Auden: Collected Poems,* ed. Edward Mendelson (New York: Vintage Books, 1991), p. 399. The poem "A Purification" is in Wendell Berry, *Collected Poems, 1957–1982* (New York: Farrar, Straus & Giroux, 1987), p. 201.

My summary of the seasons of the Christian year is based on an amalgam of sources, with an emphasis on my experiences of Lutheran worship. Many variations exist from one denomination to another, though this outline will be familiar to those who worship in the classical liturgical churches of the Western tradition. Some Protestant churches pay far less attention to liturgical seasons, though in the past generation many mainline denominations are rediscovering these rhythms. Where variations exist, readers may be interested in delving into the reasons and thereby discovering some of the special emphases of their own church. Since 1969, the liturgical reforms of Vatican II have influenced the shape of the year in all of the Western liturgical churches, but differences remain. For example, in the Roman Catholic liturgical calendar, Epiphany is a single day, while most other Western liturgical churches have adopted the Lutheran tradition of regarding Epiphany as a season that lasts until Ash Wednesday.

Two authors have recently written wonderful personal reflections on living through the Christian year: Kathleen Norris, *The Cloister Walk* (New York: Riverhead Books, 1996), and Nora Gallagher, *Things Seen and Unseen* (New York: Knopf, 1998).

CHAPTER SEVEN

On the recurrence of difference, see Noelle Oxenhandler, "Fall from Grace: How Modern Life Has Made Waiting a Desperate Act," *New Yorker,* June 16, 1997, pp. 65–68. On vacations, see Amy Harmon, "Plugged-In Nation Goes on Vacations in a New Territory," *New York Times,* July 13, 1997, pp. 1, 10.

Susan Briehl, *Come, Lord Jesus: Devotions for the Home—Advent, Epiphany, Christmas* (Minneapolis: Augsburg Fortress, 1996), offers guidance for entering these seasons of faith. Gertrude Mueller Nelson, *To Dance with God: Family Ritual and Community Celebration* (Mahwah, N.J.: Paulist Press, 1986), suggests household celebrations for the entire Christian year.

Leigh Eric Schmidt, *Consumer Rites* (Princeton, N.J.: Princeton University Press, 1995), quotes the *Dry Goods Chronicle,* April 28, 1900, on p. 18; Schmidt is the historian referred to in the discussion of "buying and selling" holidays.

On Protestant resistance to ritual, see Hughes Oliphant Old, *The Patristic Roots of Reformed Worship* (Zurich: Theologischer Verlag, 1975), p. 24; Senn, *Christian Liturgy,* pp. 362–370, 510–517; and Schmidt, *Consumer Rites,* pp. 23–26. As the twenty-first century begins, many Christians nurtured in the Reformed tradition are living through the Christian year far more fully than their forebears could have imagined. The desire for the unity of the church across denominational lines provides both an incentive and a storehouse of resources. For example, several Protestant denominations now follow the schedule of Bible readings adopted by the Roman Catholic Church in 1969, adapting it in accord with their own traditions (including Presbyterians, United Methodists, United Church of Christ, Disciples of Christ, Episcopalians, and Lutherans, though typically not every congregation within a denomination must adopt this schedule, and some congregations in other denominations may adopt it on their own). This *lectionary* follows the liturgical calendar, prescribing readings for each day in accordance with the themes of each season. Some Protestants still dissent from this calendar (which was, as they charge, developed in postapostolic times); these typically leave the choice of readings up to the minister and recognize only Easter and Christmas as holidays. The Schmemann quotation is from *For the Life of the World,* p. 53. On the biblical idea of jubilee, see Maria Harris, *Proclaim Jubilee! A Spirituality for the Twenty-First Century* (Louisville, Ky.: Westminster/John Knox, 1996), and Sharon H. Ringe, *Jesus, Liberation, and the Biblical Jubilee* (Minneapolis: Augsburg Fortress, 1985).

The quotation by Polycarp's mourners is in Senn, *Christian Liturgy,* p. 163. The story of Le Chambon is powerfully told in Philip P. Hallie, *Lest Innocent Blood Be Shed* (New York: HarperCollins, 1985). A wonderful book on how sainted ones—official and not—can sustain us in memory and hope is Elizabeth A. Johnson, *Friends of God and Prophets* (New York: Continuum, 1998).

The vespers service my family sings is Marty Haugen's *Holden Evening Prayer* (Chicago: GIA Publications, 1990).

CHAPTER EIGHT

On hospitality, Christine D. Pohl, *Making Room: Recovering Hospitality as a Christian Tradition* (Grand Rapids, Mich.: Eerdmans, 1999), quotes the woman and the monk on p. 178. The Heschel quotation is from *The Sabbath,* p. 89. Arlie Russell Hochschild calls for a "time movement" in *The Time Bind,* pp. 245–259. See also Schor, *The Overworked American,* pp. 139–165.

My reading of Psalm 90 has been informed by conversation with Esther Menn and by Joseph Sittler, "Where It Is Laid to Heart," in *The Care of the Earth and Other University Sermons* (Minneapolis: Augsburg Fortress, 1964); Walter Brueggemann, *The Message of the Psalms* (Minneapolis: Augsburg Fortress, 1984); and Claus Westermann, *The Living Psalms* (Grand Rapids, Mich.: Eerdmans, 1989).

REFERENCES

The Author

Dorothy C. Bass worked with an ecumenical and interracial group of authors to develop *Practicing Our Faith: A Way of Life for a Searching People* (Jossey-Bass, 1997), a book that addresses the contemporary hunger for a way of life that can be lived with integrity amid the many changes of our time by advocating the retrieval of twelve Christian practices: honoring the body, hospitality, household economics, saying yes and saying no, keeping sabbath, testimony, discernment, shaping communities, forgiveness, healing, dying well, and singing our lives to God.

She is director of the Valparaiso Project on the Education and Formation of People in Faith, a Lilly Endowment project based at Valparaiso University. The project sponsors a series of books and conferences aimed at developing theological, historical, and practical resources that will contribute to the authenticity and vitality of contemporary efforts in Christian education and formation.

Dr. Bass is a historian of the Christian tradition who has written many essays on religion in American culture. She serves on the board of directors of the Louisville Institute, a Lilly Endowment program for the study of American religion based at Louisville Seminary. A graduate of Wellesley College, Union Theological Seminary in New York City, and Brown University, she has taught at several colleges and theological schools. She shares her time with her husband, Mark Schwehn, who is dean of Christ College, the honors college of Valparaiso University, and their children, John and Martha.

THE AUTHOR

Index

Black church tradition, thankfulness for the day in, 19–20

Blurred boundaries: of days of the week, 59; of hours of the day, 28–29; of seasons of the year, 101–102; of time, 2, 101–102, 119, 121–122

Body care, daily honoring of, 31–33

Bondi, R., 37–38

Bonhoeffer, D., 21–23, 24, 120

Brazil, meaning of time in, 6–7

Busyness: distraction and, 35; problem of, 26; regular prayer in midst of, 37–38; of school principal, 57. *See also* Contemporary society; Time deficits

C

Calvin, J., 74

Calvinists, 67–70, 74–75

Catechumens, 88

Cathedral hours, 24

Central America, 113

Charybdis, 37

Children: importance special days of the year to, 103–104; sabbath-keeping and sports of, 73–74. *See also* Schoolchildren

Christian community: Christian year and, 105, 112; sabbath and, 52–55

Christian lens on time, 4, 12

Christian practices: for living through the year, 79–97, 99–114; for living whole lives, 115–122; for opening the gift of time, 12–14, 115–122; for receiving the day, 19–30, 31–43; for keeping the sabbath, 55–61, 63–77

Christian year, 79–97, 99–114; creative variation in, 110–111; denominational differences in, 108–109; Easter as heart of, 88–90; embrace of, in personal narrative, 83–87; feasts and fasts in, 104–108; full circle of, 90–95; integrating secular seasons with, 99–101; Jewish sources of, 87; living through the, 79–97, 99–114; meaning of, 87–95;

natural seasons and, 80; saint days in, 112–113; seasons of, 80–81, 86–95, 108–109; story of God told in, 79–97. *See also* Living through the year; Year

Christmas, 86, 95, 96; babies and, 91–92; commercialization of, 106–108; denominational differences in, 108; at Disney sites, 79–80; feast of, 104, 105; in Narnia, 79–80; winter solstice and, 80

Christmas Carol (Dickens), 107

Christmas Eve, 92

Christmas in July, 110

Chronicles of Narnia, The (Lewis), 79–80

Church committee meetings, 65–66

Church of England, 108

Church of Rome, 108

Church of the Holy Sepulchre, Jerusalem, 103

Clarke, M., 113

Clocca, 26. *See also* Bells

Clocks: awakening to, 19; invention of, 26; sabbath and, 71–72; technological and commercial role of, 26–28

Commercialism: of Christian holidays, 104, 106–108; of Christmas, 106–108; disappearance of sabbath in, 59; role of clocks in, 26–28; sabbath as rest from, 64–65; twenty-four-hour time of, 101. *See also* Global marketplace

Community life: impact of time deficits on, 8; sabbath and, 54–55; sharing time and, 119; at work *versus* at home, 8

Companions, 119

Contemporary society: clocks and, 26–28, 119; imbalances in, 2; making time in, for daily practice, 38–40; obstacles in, to keeping the sabbath, 57–61, 70, 71–73, 74–75; obstacles in, to living through the year, 96–97, 100–103; obstacles in, to living whole lives, 118–120; obstacles in, to receiving the day,

26–30; practicing receiving the day in, 26–30; quality of time in, 116–121; relevance of sabbath to, 61; resisting the time patterns of, 12–13, 118–120; round-the-clock schedule in, 2, 28–29, 101–103; sabbath-keeping in, 57–61; time deficits in, 8, 57–61, 118–120; time infrastructure of, sources of, 26–30; time-management techniques of, 1–2, 3–4, 12; time packets in, 39. *See also* Commercialism; Global marketplace

1 Corinthians 5:7, 88

Corporate downsizing, 60

Covenant, the, 49

Creation hymn, 4, 17–18, 22, 47

Creation, sabbath as rest for, 66–67

Cross, making the sign of, 20–21, 23

Cultural differences in meaning of time, 6–8

D

Daily prayer. *See* Prayer, daily

Datebooks, 1–2, 3–4, 12, 19

Day of Pentecost, 86, 91, 94–95

Day(s), 15–30, 31–43; attention in, 33–38; beginning of, at dusk, 17–18; beginning of, defining, 17–19; blurring of distinction among, 59; distractions in, 33–35; experience of, 15–16; givenness of the, 16–19; gratitude for, 19–20; interruption in, 40–43; living, a day at a time, 20–21; making time in, by saying no, 38–40; physical care during, 31–33; prayer in, 22–23, 36–38; receiving the, 18–30, 31–43; structures for, 36–38. *See also* Night and day; Prayer, daily; Receiving the day

Death: as interruption, 41–43; living fully and, 90, 115–116, 117, 120; practice of dying well and, 118; sleep and, 42–43

Depression, due to inattendance to daily self-care, 32

Deuteronomy: 5:12-15, 48; 34, 120

Dickens, C., 107

Dillard, A., 35

Disney, W., 79–80

Disney World, 79–80, 102

Distraction, 33–35; attention as antidote to, 35–36

Donovan, J., 113

Driving, on sabbath, 66

Dusk: day's beginning at, 17–18; prayer at, 25

Dutch Calvinists, 67–70, 74–75

E

Early Christians: annual festivals of, 87; monastic tradition of, 37; persecution of, 112

Easter, 11, 94, 95; date of, 80, 87; feast of, 105; meaning of, as heart of Christian year, 88–90, 94; *Pascha* in, 88–90; in personal narrative, 84–87; season of, 94

Easter Eve, 89, 114

Easter Sunrise, 90

Easter Vigil, 90, 99, 100

Eastern Orthodoxy, 87, 106, 109

Eating: daily, 32, 33; feasts and fasts and, 104–108

Egypt, Israelites' exodus from, 13, 48

El Salvador, 113

Election years, 99

Emmaus, 95

Employee, 48

Environmental protection, on sabbath, 66–67

Epiphany, 86, 91, 92, 95, 96; gift exchange on, 106–107

Episcopalians, 54

Eve of Epiphany, 92

Exercise, 32

Exodus: 15:6, 21, 48; 16, 13; 20:8-11, 47; 31:13, 49

Ezekiel, 89

F

Family life: impact of corporate time management on, 27–28; impact of time deficits on, 8; quality of time and, 117; restructuring or renouncing work for more time with, 39

Fast food, 117

Fasting, 104–108

Feasting, 104–108

Feet washing, 84

Finkenwalde, Confessing Church, 21–23

Fiscal years, 99

"Five A.M. in the Pinewoods" (Oliver), 33–35

Food, 104–108

Ford, I., 113

Forgiveness, 118

Francis, Saint, 43

Franklin, B., 27

Freedom: from bondage to yesterday, 20–21, 118; disciplines and practices for, 13–14, 118; from fear for tomorrow, 20–21, 118; sabbath-keeping as exercise of, 48–49, 60, 63, 72–73

Friends, sharing time with, 117, 119

G

Gardening, on sabbath, 67

Genesis: 1, 17, 22; 1:1-2:4a, 47; 1:1-5, 4; 2:2-3, 47

Geography of Time, A (Levine), 7

"German Christianity," 21

Gestapo, 22

Gift giving, Christmas season, 106–107

Gift of time: opening to receiving, 11–14, 115–122; perspective of, 2, 3, 4, 6; reflection on, through the year, 81, 111–115; sabbath as, 51, 55–56; throughout a lifetime, 115–122. *See also* Receiving the day

Global marketplace: round-the-clock schedule and, 28–29; vanishing sabbath and, 59. *See also* Commercialism; Contemporary society

God: activity of, in darkness, 18; as Creator, 47–48, 55; daily attention to, 36–38; as Deliverer, 48–49; image of, 48; immortality and Incarnation of, 10–11; sabbath and, 47; story of, told in Christian year, 79–97

Good Friday, 84, 85, 94, 115

Grace, saying, 33

Gratitude: for each day, 19–20; sabbath-keeping and, 118

Groundhog Day, 17

Guéranger, P., 87

Guilt and judgmentalism, 3, 8–9; about punctuality, 5–6; about use of time, 6, 8–9

Gulliver's Travels (Swift), 26–27, 119

H

Hall, D., 42

Health problems, due to inattendance to daily self-care, 32

Heschel, A., 51, 65, 118

Hitler, A., 21

Hochschild, A. R., 27–28, 119

Holy Spirit, 94–95, 109

Hosannas, 94, 96

Hospitality, 113, 117–118; sabbath and, 74

Huguenots, 113

I

Ice hockey, 73

Incarnation, 10–11, 91

Internet, round-the-clock schedule and, 28–29

Interruption: during the day, 16, 40–43; frustrations of, 40–41; mortality as, 41–43; during the week, 70

Isaiah: 35:1-10, 91; 40:1-5, 4; 60:1-4, 91

Isaiah, the prophet, 49, 91

Israelites crossing the Red Sea, 89

J

Jerusalem, 94

Jesus: birth of, in time, 10–11, 91–92; crucifixion and death of, 84, 94, 116; last supper of, 83–84, 95; Psalms as prayers of, 22, 120; on worrying about time, 20, 25

Jewish sabbath. *See* Shabbat

John: 2:1-11, 92; 20:1-18, 89

John the Baptist, 25, 91, 92

Joseph and Mary, 96

"Joy to the World," 108

Repetition, 111–113
Resistance: to contemporary time pat-
    terns, 12–13, 118–120; to keeping
    the sabbath, 74–75
Rest, on sabbath, 4, 47; from commerce,
    64–65; for creation, 66–67; from
    work, 67–70; from worry, 65. *See
    also* Sabbath
Resurrection, 20, 84–86
Rigidity, 108–110
Ritual, seasonal, 108–111
Roman Catholic calendar, 95
Roman Catholics: Lent and, 105, 108;
    saints of, 112
Roman Empire, 54, 94
Romero, O., 113
Round-the-clock time, 2, 28–29, 59,
    101–102
Rule of Saint Benedict, 32
Rules, living by, 36–37

S

Sabbath, 4; alternate days for keeping,
    75–77; children's sports on, 74–75;
    Christian community and, 52–55;
    Christian *versus* Jewish, 52; church
    committee meetings on, 65–66;
    commandment to keep, 45–47, 48,
    49; contemporary obstacles to prac-
    tice of, 57–61, 70, 71–73, 74–75; cre-
    ation song of, 47–48; creative
    variation in keeping, 63–64, 75–77;
    Dutch Calvinist keeping of, 67–69;
    first day, eighth day, 52–55; free-
    dom in, 48–49, 60, 63, 72–73; God's
    rest from creation on, 47–48, 55;
    Jewish, 49–52, 55; loneliness on,
    73–74; meaning of, 45–61, 118;
    Miriam's song of, 48–49, 52; music
    of, 46; practice of keeping, 55–61,
    63–77; receiving the gift of, 55–56;
    recreational activities on, 67, 74–75;
    relevance of, to society, 61; religious
    diversity and protection of, 58–59;
    as rest for creation, 66–67; as rest
    from commerce, 64–65; as rest from
    work, 51, 67–70; as rest from worry,

65–66; on Saturday and Sunday
    evening, 76; social protection of, de-
    cline in, 58–59; specific practices for,
    63–77; Sunday, Christian tradition
    of, 54, 75–76; working on, 71–73;
    worship on, 52–55, 56, 70–71
Saints and martyrs, 112–113
San Fernando Cathedral, 52–54, 56
San Francisco Bay Area, synagogue in,
    50
Schmemann, A., 76, 109
School principal job, 57
School season, 99, 104
Schoolchildren: bells and, 4–5; datebooks
    of, 1–2. *See also* Children
Schor, J., 59–60, 64–65
Schütz, H., 84
Scrooge, Ebenezer, 107
Scylla, 37
Searle, M., 90–91
Seasons, 79–81, 108; blurring of, 96–97,
    100–102; of the Christian year,
    80–81, 86–95, 108–109; secular,
    99–100; spinning of, 80–81; story-
    telling and, 81–82. *See also* Christ-
    ian year; Living through the year;
    Year
Second Vatican Council, 105
Self-care, daily, 31–33
Sesame Street, 103
7-Eleven, 101
Shabbat, 49–52, 55; day of the week of,
    49, 75, 76; Jewish identity and,
    51–52; keeping, in contemporary
    culture, 50; legal protection of, 59;
    observances on, 51; origins of, 49;
    practices of, 49–50; proscription
    against driving on, 66; proscription
    against timepieces on, 71; proscrip-
    tion against work on, 51; shalom in,
    51
Shadrach, 89
Shaw, J., 5–6
Shopping, sabbath as rest from, 64–65
Sidewalk tag, 73–74
"Silent Night," 92
Sin, wasting time as, 6

on sabbath, 71–73; pressures to, 60; resting from the thought of, 65; restructuring or renouncing, for more time, 39; round-the-clock, 28–29, 102, 103; sabbath as rest from, 51, 67–70; test of, 22–23; time demands of, 57–58, 59–61, 117, 119; time imbalances in, 2, 4

Working poor, 2, 60

Worry: living this day and, 20–21; sabbath as rest from, 65–66

Worship, sabbath: authentic, 56; Christian community gathering and, 52–55, 56; clocking, 71–72; joyful, 70–71

and fasts in, 104–108; God's story in, 79–97, 99–114; guidance for living through the, 103–104; motions of, 81–82; obstacles to living through the, 96–97, 100–103; practice of living through the, 79–97, 99–114; repetition in, 111–113; roundness of, 81–82, 111–113; seasons in, 79–81, 99–101. *See also* Christian year; Living through the year

Yesterday, freedom from bondage to, 20–21, 118

Y

Z

This page constitutes a continuation of the copyright page.